MILADY'S STANDARD ESTHETICS:
Fundamentals Workbook

10th Edition

Jeryl Spear

Australia • Brazil • Japan • Korea • Mexico • Singapore • Spain • United Kingdom • United States

Milady's Standard Esthetics: Fundamentals Workbook, Tenth Edition
Jeryl Spear

President, Milady: Dawn Gerrain

Publisher: Erin O'Connor

Acquisitions Editor: Martine Edwards

Product Manager: Jessica Burns

Editorial Assistant: Mike Spring

Director of Beauty Industry Relations: Sandra Bruce

Marketing Manager: Gerard McAvey

Marketing Coordinator: Matthew McGuire

Production Director: Wendy Troeger

Senior Content Project Manager: Nina Tucciarelli

Art Director: Joy Kocsis

Technology Project Manager: Sandy Charette

© 2009, 2004 Milady, Cengage Learning

ALL RIGHTS RESERVED. No part of this work covered by the copyright herein may be reproduced, transmitted, stored, or used in any form or by any means graphic, electronic, or mechanical, including but not limited to photocopying, recording, scanning, digitizing, taping, Web distribution, information networks, or information storage and retrieval systems, except as permitted under Section 107 or 108 of the 1976 United States Copyright Act, without the prior written permission of the publisher.

> For product information and technology assistance, contact us at
> **Professional & Career Group Customer Support, 1-800-648-7450**
> For permission to use material from this text or product,
> submit all requests online at **cengage.com/permissions**
> Further permissions questions can be e-mailed to
> **permissionrequest@cengage.com**

Library of Congress Control Number: 2007941007

ISBN-13: 978-1-4283-1894-6

ISBN-10: 1-4283-1894-1

Milady
5 Maxwell Drive
Clifton Park, NY 12065-2919
USA

Cengage Learning products are represented in Canada by Nelson Education, Ltd.

For your lifelong learning solutions, visit **delmar.cengage.com**

Visit our corporate website at **cengage.com**

Notice to the Reader
Publisher does not warrant or guarantee any of the products described herein or perform any independent analysis in connection with any of the product information contained herein. Publisher does not assume, and expressly disclaims, any obligation to obtain and include information other than that provided to it by the manufacturer. The reader is expressly warned to consider and adopt all safety precautions that might be indicated by the activities described herein and to avoid all potential hazards. By following the instructions contained herein, the reader willingly assumes all risks in connection with such instructions. The publisher makes no representations or warranties of any kind, including but not limited to, the warranties of fitness for particular purpose or merchantability, nor are any such representations implied with respect to the material set forth herein, and the publisher takes no responsibility with respect to such material. The publisher shall not be liable for any special, consequential, or exemplary damages resulting, in whole or part, from the readers' use of, or reliance upon, this material.

Table of Contents

How to Use this Workbook   v

CHAPTER 1   History and Career Opportunities in Esthetics   1
CHAPTER 2   Your Professional Image   4
CHAPTER 3   Communicating for Success   8
CHAPTER 4   Infection Control: Principles and Practice   14
CHAPTER 5   General Anatomy and Physiology   19
CHAPTER 6   Basics of Chemistry   35
CHAPTER 7   Basics of Electricity   42
CHAPTER 8   Basics of Nutrition   48
CHAPTER 9   Physiology and Histology of the Skin   52
CHAPTER 10   Disorders and Diseases of the Skin   57
CHAPTER 11   Skin Analysis   69
CHAPTER 12   Skin Care Products: Chemistry, Ingredients, and Selection   77
CHAPTER 13   The Treatment Room   86
CHAPTER 14   Basic Facials   91
CHAPTER 15   Facial Massage   97
CHAPTER 16   Facial Machines   100
CHAPTER 17   Hair Removal   107
CHAPTER 18   Advanced Topics and Treatments   112
CHAPTER 19   The World of Makeup   121
CHAPTER 20   Career Planning   139
CHAPTER 21   The Skin Care Business   149
CHAPTER 22   Selling Products and Services   156

How to Use this Workbook

This workbook has been especially designed to meet the needs, interests, and abilities of students receiving training for a career in esthetics, the art of skin care. It has been organized to be used in conjunction with *Milady's Standard Esthetics: Fundamentals,* 10th Edition.

The material presented here has been prepared in accordance with the accepted methods of vocational training that are approved by state licensing organizations.

1. Assignment of the Lesson

    Pages to be read and studied are listed at the top of the page.

2. Learning the Lesson

    The student writes the answers in the workbook, consulting the text and glossary located in the back of *Milady's Standard Esthetics: Fundamentals,* 10th Edition.

3. Correction of the Lesson

    Answers may be corrected and rated during class discussions.

4. Review of the Lesson

    Various tests emphasize the essential facts and measure the student's progress.

Date: _____

Rating: _____

Text pages: 1–17

CHAPTER 1

History and Career Opportunities in Esthetics

TOPIC 1: BRIEF HISTORY OF SKIN CARE

1. In ancient times, people around the world used pigments on their hair, skin, and nails made from materials such as _____.

2. Which ancient people were the first to use cosmetics in an extravagant way? _____

3. Which ancient people used cosmetics primarily for cleansing and maintenance of the skin, hair, teeth, and bodily health? _____

4. The words *cosmetics* and *cosmetology* are derived from which language? _____

5. People of this ancient civilization are famous for their public baths. _____

6. The period in European history between classical antiquity and the Renaissance is called the _____.

7. Women of status bathed in strawberries and milk and used various extravagant cosmetic preparations during which age? _____

8. One of the most austere periods in history, during which the use of makeup was discouraged, spanned the reign of _____.

9. Which important antiaging products were introduced in the twentieth century? _____

10. The beginning of the twenty-first century ushered in the science _____ a microscopic approach to skin care ingredients.

11. The birth of which type of spa in the late twentieth century changed the skin care industry? _____

Rapid Review Test

Date: _____

Rating: _____

Word Review

| nanotechnology | alpha hydroxy acids | myrrh | Botox® |
| medical spa | beta hydroxy acids | aromatics | Retin-A® |

1. The Egyptians used cosmetics for religious ceremonies, in preparing the deceased for burial, and for their _____.

2. The Hebrews used myrrh and pomegranate as _____.

3. During which period did women tweeze their eyebrows and hairline to show a greater expanse of forehead? _____

4. The words *cosmetics* and *cosmetology* are derived from the Greek word _____.
5. During which age did the women use honey, oatmeal, eggs, milk, fruits, and vegetables to make beauty masks? _____
6. Steam therapy, body scrubs, massage, and other physical therapies were all available at ancient _____.
7. The art of manipulating materials on an atomic or molecular scale is called _____.
8. The birth of the _____ has taken center stage to facilitate and support the cosmetic surgery phenomenon.
9. Many compounding pharmacies have taken a market share of the cosmetic industry by offering advanced preparations that can contain _____ for topical use.
10. What type of product line can estheticians create to meet the branding needs of a salon or spa? _____

TOPIC 2: CAREER PATHS FOR AN ESTHETICIAN

1. Esthetics comes from the Greek word _____, meaning _____.
2. Estheticians offer skin care treatments and sell cosmetics, but cannot prescribe _____ or give medical _____.
3. An esthetician is a person devoted to, or professionally occupied with, the _____ and _____ of the skin.
4. Estheticians in a salon or day spa are skin care _____ and _____
5. Medical esthetics involves the integration of _____ and _____.
6. A good makeup artist is skillful at _____ a person's more attractive features and _____ less attractive features.
7. Cosmetic manufacturers often hire _____ to call on salons or stores to sell products and help build clienteles.
8. Cosmetics _____ estimate the amount of stock an operation will need over a particular period, and keep records of product purchases and sales.
9. Educators may teach esthetics in _____, _____, _____, or _____ schools.
10. Skin care products are continuing to become more _____ and have more efficient _____ that penetrate deeper into the skin.
11. Skin care in general is becoming more _____ than corrective.

Rapid Review Test

Date: _____

Rating: _____

1. Match the following terms with the most accurate description:

Term	Answer	Description
a) Estheticians in a spa or salon	_____	1. Demonstrate products to potential customers
b) Medical aestheticians	_____	2. Demonstrate products, cashiering
c) Salespeople/Sales managers	_____	3. Serve the traveling public
d) Makeup artists	_____	4. Work for a magazine or newspaper
e) Manufacturer's reps	_____	5. Travel frequently; estimate stock for customers
f) Researchers	_____	6. Perform waxing and facial services

g) Cosmetics buyers _____ 7. Work in public, industrial, vocational schools

h) Esthetics writers/editors _____ 8. Conduct regular salon inspections

i) Travel industry _____ 9. Determine the safety of products

j) Educators _____ 10. Work for television and movie productions

k) State licensing examiners _____ 11. Camouflage makeup, advanced treatments

l) State board members _____ 12. Conduct licensure examinations

2. The branch of anatomical science dealing with the health and well-being of the skin is called _____.

3. The field that integrates surgical and esthetic treatments is called _____.

4. The medical setting in which patients receive both spa services and medical procedures is called a _____.

5. When you apply makeup to cover scars or congenital defects, you are performing _____.

6. A makeup artist who works in a mortuary is skilled at _____.

7. The travel industry is now using _____ for airport and in-flight services, as well as on cruise ships.

8. Manufacturers often employ estheticians as _____ who conduct seminars and workshops, display products at conventions, and talk with teachers about the merits of the products.

9. Licensing exams are conducted and licenses are granted by _____.

10. Americans born between the years 1946 and 1964 are known as _____.

11. The U.S. Department of Labor predicts the rapid growth of _____ and a growing demand for practitioners licensed to provide a _____.

Date: _____

Rating: _____

Text pages: 18–32

CHAPTER 2
Your Professional Image

TOPIC 1: YOUR PROFESSIONAL APPEARANCE

1. The impression you project as a person engaged in the profession of esthetics is your _____ _____.

2. Your professional image is made up of your _____ and your _____ in the workplace.

3. If you do not _____ your clients will assume that you cannot make them _____.

4. Personal hygiene is the daily maintenance of _____ and _____ through certain sanitary practices.

5. Personal hygiene consists of certain basic tasks, including:
   a) _____
   b) _____
   c) _____
   d) _____
   e) _____
   f) _____
   g) _____

6. Your posture, movements, and the way you walk make up your _____.

7. Good posture can prevent _____ and other physical problems.

8. To achieve good standing posture, practice these six steps:
   a) _____
   b) _____
   c) _____
   d) _____
   e) _____
   f) _____

9. To achieve good sitting posture, take these four steps:
   a) _____
   b) _____
   c) _____
   d) _____

TOPIC 2: YOUR PROFESSIONAL IMAGE

1. You may not be able to change an inborn characteristic or a genetic trait, but you can change your _____.

2. People who are committed to doing a good job have a strong _____.

3. Name the ingredients of a healthy, well-developed attitude:

   a) _____   e) _____
   b) _____   f) _____
   c) _____   g) _____
   d) _____   h) _____

4. If you consistently practice good _____ techniques, you can decrease the potential for conflict with clients and coworkers.

5. Establishing a good _____ involves being trustworthy, reliable, hard-working, respectful and supportive of others.

6. An important rule when talking with clients is to never engage in _____.

7. When dealing with difficult people at work, it is important to remember that you are in a _____ and your standards for dealing with others must be _____.

8. Counting to 10 and thinking before you speak, and not engaging in a no-win situation or argument, are _____ to help handle conflicts as they arise in the workplace.

9. Ethics are the principles of _____ and _____ as expressed through personality, human relations skills, and (professional image).

10. The way you handle yourself and behave _____ determines whether you can attain and sustain success.

Rapid Review Test

Date: _____

Rating: _____

1. When you do not share what your clients have told you in confidence, you are showing _____.

2. Your outlook, or _____, affects the way you live your life.

3. Showing understanding, empathy, and acceptance for the feelings of others is a sign of _____.

4. Self-control is an important aspect of _____.

5. The skill of _____ involves being tactful in your dealings with other people.

6. Teamwork is essential to developing a positive _____ in a salon environment.

TOPIC 3: PROFESSIONAL ETHICS

1. The moral principles that we live and work by are called _____.

2. The first step in establishing credibility as an esthetician is obtaining the appropriate _____.

3. General guidelines for becoming a confident, trustworthy professional are:

   a) _____
   b) _____
   c) _____
   d) _____
   e) _____
   f) _____
   g) _____

h) _____
i) _____
4. Maintain your integrity by making sure your behavior and actions match your _____.

Rapid Review Test

Date: _____

Rating: _____

Word Review

| ethics | FDA | unethical | integrity |
| unbiased | confidentialities | state board | NCEA |

1. You should join and participate in professional organizations that take a(n) _____ approach to esthetics.
2. _____ are the moral principles by which we live and work.
3. Estheticians must maintain client _____.
4. The mission of the _____ is to represent the esthetics profession by defining and conveying standards of practice.
4. In cosmetology, each _____ sets the ethical standards that all estheticians who work in that state must follow.
5. The function of the _____ is to protect the consumer, including preventing the public from being duped by false claims and advertising.
6. If you believe a client needs products and additional services for healthy skin maintenance, it would be _____ not to give the client that information.
7. Maintaining your _____ includes endorsing your employer's price structure and other policies.

TOPIC 4: LIFE SKILLS

1. Some of the most important life skills are:

   a) _____
   b) _____
   c) _____
   d) _____
   e) _____
   f) _____
   g) _____
   h) _____
   i) _____
   j) _____
   k) _____
   l) _____
   m) _____

2. Your self-esteem is based on your _____.
3. Time management is essential to living a _____.
4. A winner decides on a goal, makes a plan, and _____.
5. Planning to open a salon in 5 to 10 years is one example of a _____.
6. In the esthetics business, time is _____.
7. Making a to-do list, from the most-to-least important, is a way of _____.
8. You will find it easier to complete your tasks if you limit your activities and do not _____
_____.
9. At the end of the day, you should start _____.
10. When combined with additional consultation and retail responsibilities, the average treatment time generally totals about _____.

Rapid Review Test

Date: _____

Review: _____

Word Review

self-critical	procrastination	perfectionism	competence
visualize	self-image	maturity	principles

Match the following terms with their descriptions below.

long-term	respect	game plan	separate	follow-up
reward	time	success	short-term	self-esteem

1. _____ goals are measured in large sections of time, such as 2 years, 5 years, or even longer.
2. When you treat people well, they will _____ you.
3. _____ your personal life from your work life.
4. Invest in yourself by coming up with a _____.
5. If we are able to manage our _____ wisely, we can live more fulfilling lives.
6. _____ goals are usually those you want to accomplish within a year at the most.
7. Leave time in your schedule for important _____ phone calls.
8. _____ yourself for a job well done.
9. The road to _____ is best reached with a clear plan that will lead you where you want to go.
10. When people respect you, it helps build your _____.

Date: _____

Rating: _____

Text pages: 33–54

CHAPTER 3
Communicating for Success

TOPIC 1: HUMAN RELATIONS

1. The ability to understand people is especially important in esthetics, where _____ is central to success.
2. The best way to understand others is to begin with a firm understanding of _____.
3. When we create an atmosphere where customers and staff have confidence in us, we will get the _____ we deserve.
4. When we feel _____, we are happy, calm and confident; when we feel _____, we become worried, anxious and overwhelmed.
5. Human beings are _____ animals.
6. To become skilled in human relations, learn to _____ of situations that could otherwise drain both your time and your energy.
7. _____ instead of reacting to situations.
8. _____. When you do, you trust your judgment, uphold your own values, and stick to what you believe is right.
9. _____ and listen more.
10. You can usually calm difficult clients by _____. This tactic works nine times out of ten.

The Golden Rules of Human Relations

11. Communicate from your heart; _____ from your head.
12. Learn to ask for help when you are _____.
13. Show people you care by _____ to them and trying to understand their _____.
14. Being right is different from being _____.
15. Listening is the best _____.

Rapid Review Test

Date: _____

Rating: _____

Word Review

Match the following terms with their descriptions below.

human relations	interact	give	yourself
understanding	first	understand	communicate

1. The ability to _____ people is the key to operating effectively in many professions.
2. Most of your interactions will depend on your ability to _____ successfully with a wide range of people.
3. A fundamental factor in _____ has to do with how secure we are feeling.
4. When we feel secure, we like to _____ with other people.
5. Believe in _____.
6. Human relations can be rewarding or frustrating; it all depends on how willing you are to _____.
7. Part of giving a good service is taking care of yourself _____.
8. If there is something you do not understand, ask a question to gain _____.

The Golden Rules of Human Relations
1. Treat people in a way that allows them to maintain their _____.
2. Balance your service to others with _____.
3. Listening is the best _____.
4. Be a _____ and partner with your clients.
5. Be _____ by demonstrating your support in difficult times.
6. Make _____ when you are wrong.

TOPIC 2: COMMUNICATION BASICS
1. _____ is the act of successfully sharing information between two or more people.
2. When communicating, many times it is not what we _____, but rather how we _____.
3. When you and your client are both _____ clearly about an upcoming service, your chances of pleasing that person soar.
4. One of the most important communications you will have with a client is the _____ _____.
5. Always approach a new client with a _____.
6. You will need to allow time in your schedule for a _____ minute consultation.
7. Having a client sign a _____ is standard practice for more aggressive treatments.
8. When introducing a consent form to clients, take time to review all the steps involved in the process, and carefully explain any _____ instructions that may be necessary.

Rapid Review Test
Date: _____

Rating: _____

1. Describe the corresponding negative nonverbal cues.
    a) A pleasant tone of voice: _____
    b) A smile: _____
    c) Appropriate body distance: _____
    d) Good eye contact: _____
    e) A moderate tone of voice: _____
    f) An even rate of speech: _____

2. Word Review

Match the following terms with their descriptions below.

| impressions | interactions | powerful | intake form |
| tour | yourself | introduce | needs |

a) Names are _____ and they are meant to be used.

b) Time spent with a client is meant for her _____ and not yours.

c) Be _____.

d) Set aside a few minutes to give clients a _____ of the salon.

e) Always _____ yourself when first meeting a new client.

f) Introduce clients to people they may have _____ with while in the salon.

g) First impressions are often the most _____ impressions.

h) An _____ is also called a client questionnaire.

TOPIC 3: THE CLIENT CONSULTATION

1. The client consultation is the verbal communication that determines the _____.

2. Some professionals skip the client consultation altogether, or they make time for it only on the client's first visit. These professionals are making a _____.

3. Most importantly, a consultation helps to eliminate the potential for _____.

4. Each client is an individual with a _____ agenda.

5. To determine the best outcome, you will want to gather as much information as possible without _____ or _____.

6. When conducting a consultation, the information that the client provides is considered _____ and should be held strictly _____.

7. Before-and-after photos are an excellent way to demonstrate the _____.

8. If you decide to perform a treatment that goes against your best judgment and causes harm to a client, _____.

9. _____ counts for a lot in a business that is concerned with appearances.

10. When giving a consultation, your work area should be _____.

11. Throughout the consultation, and especially after deciding on a course of action, make notes on the _____.

10-Step Consultation Form

12. Every complete consultation needs to be structured in such a way that you cover _____ that consistently lead to a successful conclusion.

13. Listening to the client and then repeating, in your own words, what you think the client is telling you is known as _____.

14. Once the service is finished and the client has let you know whether she is satisfied, take a few more minutes to record the results on the _____.

15. Always supply your client with a _____ of the products and treatments you have suggested, along with specific directions for _____ and recommended time frames for _____.

Rapid Review Test

Date: _____

Rating: _____

1. Estheticians can be held liable for a breach of _____.
2. The _____ is the most important interaction that you will have with a client.
3. Information gathered during a consultation will help create a _____ relationship.
4. For your time to be well spent during the client consultation, it is important to be _____.
5. A _____ should be part of every single service and salon visit.
6. Important information to gather during a consultation that could adversely affect a treatment includes _____ _____.
7. _____ are an excellent way to demonstrate the results of a product or treatment.
8. Vendor pamphlets that contain before and after photos are often a better resource for demonstrating the details of _____.
9. As part of your consultation, have any _____ that you will use to describe the benefits, at the ready.
10. Throughout the consultation, and especially once a course of action is decided on, _____ on the intake form.

Complete the following sentences that describe the 10-Step Consultation Method.

1. _____ the intake form.
2. _____ your client's current goals and objectives.
3. Ask your clients what _____ she is currently using, and how much time she prefers spending on her skin care regimen.
4. Using a magnifying loupe and/or Wood's lamp, _____ the client's skin.
5. Ask your client about her career and personal _____.
6. _____ the various treatment options.
7. Once you have enough information to make valid suggestions, narrow the treatment options based on _____.
8. Proper _____ protection should be part of every consultation.
9. _____ everything that you have agreed upon.

TOPIC 4: SPECIAL ISSUES IN COMMUNICATION

1. Although you may do everything in your power to communicate effectively, you will sometimes encounter situations that are _____.
2. When handling tardy clients, you must know and abide by the _____.
3. If your client arrives late, and you still have the time to take her without jeopardizing other clients' appointments, let your client know _____, even though she is tardy.
4. When you, as the professional, get involved with a scheduling mix-up, you must always be _____ and never _____ about who is correct.
5. Once in a while you will encounter a client who is dissatisfied with a service. The way you and the salon handle this difficult situation will have lasting effects on _____.
6. When trying to find out why the client is unhappy, always ask for _____.
7. If it is possible to change what a client dislikes, _____.

8. When dealing with difficult clients, do not take offensive words or actions _____.
9. Learn to censor your dialogue and _____.
10. Use language that evokes a _____ response.
11. Acknowledge concerns, and state how you can _____.
12. Sometimes when a client forms a bond of trust with her esthetician, she may have a hard time differentiating between _____.
13. Your job and your relationship with your clients are very specific: the goal is to _____ clients with their skin care needs.

Rapid Review Test

Date: _____

Rating: _____

Word Review

Match the following terms with their descriptions below.

habitually	blame	respected	maturely
last	promptness	reschedule	reschedule

a) Generally, if clients are more than 15 minutes late, they should be asked to _____.
b) As you get to know your clients, you will learn who is _____ late.
c) Even when you know that a client is wrong, take the _____ if it makes her happy.
d) Your clients deserve and expect your _____.
e) Letting your next appointment know that you are running late may not make her happy, but it will make her feel informed and _____.
f) If a client is too upset to handle a situation _____, it may be easier for her to deal with someone else.

TOPIC 5: IN-SALON COMMUNICATION

1. In a work environment, you will not have the opportunity to handpick your _____.
2. Regardless of whether you like a colleague, you should treat that person with _____.
3. To learn and grow, you must make every effort to remain _____ and _____ being pulled into spats and cliques.
4. While honesty is always the best policy, using _____ is never a good idea.
5. If you have a problem with a colleague, the best way to resolve it is to speak with him or her _____.
6. Keep your private life _____.
7. When you need to speak with your manager about some issue or problem, think of some possible _____ beforehand.
8. Be open to _____ criticism.

Communicating during an Employee Evaluation

9. Well-run salons will make every effort to have frequent and thorough employee _____.
10. Many salons are now drafting _____ that clearly identify their human resource policies on wage increases and the protocol for advancement.

Rapid Review Test

Date: _____

Rating: _____

Word Review

Match the following terms with their descriptions below.

resolves	objective	respectfully	honest	evaluation
disrespectfully	techniques	neutral	conflict	performance

a) Regardless of whether you like certain colleagues, it's smart to hone in on their talents and _____.

b) Instead of taking sides when controversy is brewing in your salon, you should remain _____.

c) Speaking to, or gossiping with, others about someone never _____ a problem.

d) Many people use the excuse of being _____ as a license to say anything to anyone.

e) If you find yourself in a position where you are at odds with a coworker, seek the help of someone who can remain _____.

f) When someone behaves _____ in a salon, it affects the entire team.

g) Because the salon is your workplace, it must be treated _____ and carefully.

h) Do whatever you have to do to avoid being drawn into a _____.

i) The employee _____ is the perfect time to ask when you can take on more services or increase your pay scale.

j) An employee evaluation is meant to help you _____ your work performance.

13

Date: _____

Rating: _____

Text pages: 55–90

CHAPTER 4
Infection Control: Principles and Practice

TOPIC 1: PRINCIPLES OF INFECTION

1. Why should estheticians study bacteria? _____
   _____.

2. Tiny plant or animal cells that cannot be seen with the naked eye are called _____.

3. Bacteria are also known as _____ or _____.

4. _____ bacteria help the body breakdown food, protect against infection, and stimulate the immune system.

5. _____ bacteria are considered harmful because they may cause disease or infection when they invade the body.

6. What are the shapes of the following bacteria?

    a) cocci: _____

    b) bacilli: _____

    c) spirilla: _____

7. Which bacteria cause the following diseases?

    a) pustules and boils: _____

    b) tuberculosis: _____

    c) strep throat: _____

    d) Lyme disease: _____

    e) pneumonia: _____

8. Identify the bacteria illustrated below:

    a) _____

    b) _____

    c) _____

a.   b.   c.

9. The life cycle of bacteria is made up of these two phases:
   a) _____
   b) _____
10. To survive difficult conditions such as famine or unsuitable temperatures, certain bacteria form _____ outer shell.
11. What is one important difference between viruses and bacteria? _____
_____
12. Viruses are generally resistant to _____.
13. Hepatitis and HIV are _____ pathogens.
14. In the salon setting, the HIV virus can be transmitted by _____
_____.
15. _____ is a viral disease characterized by liver inflammation.
16. In what ways does the body fight infection?
   a) _____
   b) _____
   c) _____
   d) _____
17. Pathogenic bacteria and viruses that are carried through the body in blood or body fluids are called _____.
18. When pathogenic bacteria or viruses invade the body, _____ may occur.
19. A disease that spreads by contact from one person to another is _____.
20. A _____ infection is confined to a particular part of the body.
21. When bacteria or viruses are carried throughout the body, a _____ infection results.
22. _____ live in or on another living organism, and draw their nourishment from this organism.
23. Ringworm is a vegetable (plant) parasite or _____.
24. There are two types of parasites; those living _____ a host and those living _____.
25. The ability of the body to resist infection is called _____.
26. _____ is a set of guidelines that requires employees to assume that all human blood and body fluids are infectious.

Rapid Review Test

Date: _____

Rating: _____

Word Review

Insert the correct term in the space provided.

acquired	HIV	nonpathogenic
hepatitis	host	staphylococci
fungi	inoculation	scabies
general infection	microscope	spores
hepatitis	natural	viruses

1. Most bacteria are classified as _____.
2. Some pathogens protect themselves from harsh conditions by forming _____.

15

3. The common cold, smallpox, and AIDS are all caused by _____.
4. Bacteria become visible when observed under a _____.
5. _____ is the virus that causes AIDS.
6. A disease caused by a virus similar to HIV, but more easily contracted, is called _____.
7. The _____ virus is present in all body fluids.
8. _____ are among the most common human bacteria.
9. AIDS is a type of _____ infection.
10. Parasites cannot live without a _____.
11. Molds, mildews, and yeasts are all types of _____.
12. The skin disease caused by the itch mite is _____.
13. _____ immunity is an inherited resistance to disease.
14. _____ immunity is developed after the body overcomes a disease.
15. Acquired immunity can also be developed through _____ or after the body overcomes a disease.

TOPIC 2: PRINCIPLES OF PREVENTION

1. The federal agency that enforces safety and health standards in the workplace is _____.
2. The Occupational Safety and Health Act of 1970 regulates employee exposure to _____ substances.
3. Most objects or surfaces in your surroundings are _____, which means they have microorganisms in or on them.
4. The three main levels of decontamination are:
    a) _____
    b) _____
    c) _____
5. _____ kills all microorganisms, including bacterial spores.
6. An autoclave sterilizes tools by using _____ under pressure.
7. Disinfection kills most microorganisms on hard, _____ surfaces.
8. Disinfection does not kill _____.
9. _____ should not be used on human skin, hair, or nails.
10. The _____ registers different types of disinfectants.
11. Manufacturers are required to provide information about their products in a _____.
12. A disinfectant that is effective against the pseudomonas bacteria is called _____.
13. Any implement that comes into contact with blood or body fluids must be disinfected in an EPA-registered tuberculocidal disinfectant or a disinfectant that kills _____ and _____ virus.
14. Which disinfectants have the following characteristics?
    a) _____: not a legal disinfectant in most states
    b) _____: nontoxic, odorless, and fast acting
    c) _____: effective laundry additive
    d) _____: caustic poison
15. You should always wear _____ and _____ when mixing disinfectants.
16. An important rule when mixing disinfectants is to add _____ to _____.

17. The purpose of wet sanitizers is to _____.
18. Any item used on a client must be _____ or _____.
19. _____ or _____ may grow on unwashed laundry that has been left in a laundry cart.
20. Touching an object, such as the skin, and then touching another object or product with the same hand or utensil, results in _____.
21. _____ supplies and implements are thrown away after use.
22. Products used in skin care treatments should be removed from their containers with a _____.
23. Use _____, _____, or a _____ to remove implements from disinfectants.
24. The lowest level of decontamination is _____.
25. _____ may kill, retard, or prevent the growth of bacteria, but they are not classified as disinfectants.
26. Disposable lancets should be disposed of in a _____.
27. Nonporous tools such as tweezers and scissors that have not come in contact with blood should be decontaminated by complete immersion in an EPA-registered, hospital-grade disinfectant that is:
    a) _____
    b) _____
    c) _____
    d) _____
28. Universal Precautions require that employers and employees assume that all human _____ and _____ are infectious for HIV, HBV, and other bloodborne pathogens.

Rapid Review Test

Date: _____

Rating: _____

Word Review

Insert the correct term in the space provided.

aseptic	dry heat	pathogens
asymptomatic	efficacy	sodium hypochlorite
contaminants	formalin	disinfected
decontamination	glass electrodes	antiseptic
double-bagging	immersion	Universal Precautions

1. Dirt, oils, makeup on a brush, or lotion on a cotton pad are all _____.
2. Removing pathogens from tools and surfaces is called _____.
3. Methods of sterilization include the autoclave and _____.
4. Tools that come into contact with blood or other bodily fluids must be _____.
5. Items such as _____ cannot be sterilized in an autoclave, because they will break.
6. Any disinfectant used in a salon must have the correct _____ or effectiveness against pathogens.
7. _____ was used as a disinfectant in the past, but it is no longer considered safe for salon use.
8. The chemical term for _____ is (sodium hypochlorite).

9. Proper disinfection procedure requires complete _____ in disinfectant for the required amount of time.
10. Handling sterilized and disinfected equipment and supplies so they are not contaminated until they are used on a client is called an _____ procedure.
11. In a blood spill, after cleaning the wound, apply an _____ to the wound.
12. Contaminated disposable objects such as cotton balls should be discarded by _____.
13. Sanitizing means significantly reducing the number of _____ on a surface.
14. OSHA prescribes the use of _____ as the approach to infection control.
15. A client who is _____ shows no symptoms or signs of infection.

Date: _____

Rating: _____

Text pages: 91–126

CHAPTER 5
General Anatomy and Physiology

TOPIC 1: CELLS

1. The study of the functions and activities performed by the body's structures is called _____.
2. The study of body structures that can be seen with the naked eye, and what they are made up of, is called _____.
3. _____ is the science of the minute structures of organic tissues.
4. What is a cell? _____
5. Describe protoplasm. _____
6. Match the following cell structures to their definitions:

| cell membrane | cytoplasm | nucleus |

   a) _____: all the protoplasm of a cell except that which is in the nucleus
   b) _____: structure that encloses the protoplasm
   c) _____: dense protoplasm found in the center of the cell

7. Cells divide into two identical cells called _____.
8. Cells reproduce by a process known as _____.
9. Constructive metabolism, in which larger molecules are built from smaller ones, is called _____.
10. The phase of metabolism in which complex compounds are broken down into smaller ones is called _____.
11. Match each of these examples of tissue with its tissue type:
    a) _____: muscular tissue
    b) _____: connective tissue
    c) _____: nerve tissue
    d) _____: epithelial tissue
12. Match each of these organs with its function:

| heart | lungs | stomach | kidneys | liver |

   a) _____ supplies oxygen to the blood.
   b) _____ removes toxic products of digestion.
   c) _____ excrete water and waste products.
   d) _____ digests food.
   e) _____ circulates the blood.

13. List the eleven major body systems:
    a) _____
    b) _____
    c) _____
    d) _____
    e) _____
    f) _____
    g) _____
    h) _____
    i) _____
    j) _____
    k) _____

Rapid Review Test

Date: _____

Rating: _____

1. Most cells reproduce through a process known as _____.
2. _____ is a chemical process whereby cells are nourished and carry out their activities.
3. Anabolism and catabolism are the two phases of _____.
4. _____ is the tissue that supports, protects, and binds together other body tissues.
5. Bone tissue is composed of several types of bone cells that are embedded in a web of _____.
6. A/an _____ is a group of tissues that perform a specific function.
7. A _____ is made up of organs working together to perform one or more functions.
8. The endocrine system is made up of specialized _____.
9. The brain and spinal cord are part of the _____.

TOPIC 2: THE SKELETAL SYSTEM

1. How many bones are there in the skeletal system? _____
2. Bones are connected by movable and immovable _____.
3. Name the five primary functions of the skeletal system:
    a) _____
    b) _____
    c) _____
    d) _____
    e) _____
4. Elbows and knees are examples of _____ joints.
5. The skull is divided into two parts: the _____ and the _____.

6. Use the following two illustrations to identify the bones of the cranium and face in the corresponding spaces.

a) _____

b) _____

c) _____

d) _____

e) _____

f) _____

g) _____

h) _____

i) _____

j) _____

k) _____

l) _____

m) _____

n) _____

21

7. Match these cranial bones with their descriptions:

| ethmoid bone | occipital bone | sphenoid bone |
| frontal bone | parietal bones | temporal bones |

   a) _____ joins all the bones of the cranium together.
   b) _____ forms the forehead.
   c) _____ hindmost bone of the skull.
   d) _____ form the sides of the head in the ear region.
   e) _____ form the sides and crown of the cranium.
   f) _____ is light, spongy bone between the eye sockets.

8. Identify the bones of the neck, shoulder, and back in the corresponding spaces.

   a) _____
   b) _____
   c) _____
   d) _____
   e) _____
   f) _____
   g) _____

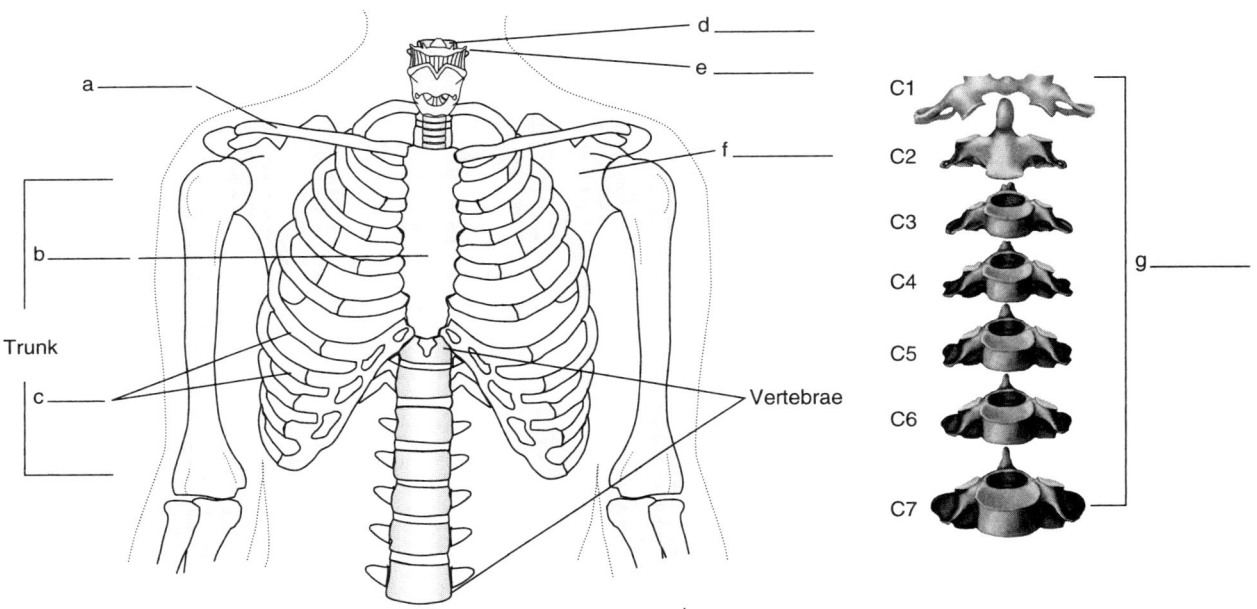

9. The _____ is a U-shaped bone at the base of the tongue.
10. How many pairs of ribs are there in the thorax? _____
11. Match these bones of the shoulder, arm, and hand with their definitions:

carpus	clavicle	humerus
metacarpus	phalanges	radius
scapula	ulna	

   a) _____: shoulder blade
   b) _____: palm

c) _____: collarbone
d) _____: inner, larger bone of the forearm
e) _____: uppermost, largest bone of the arm
f) _____: finger bones
g) _____: wrist
h) _____: smaller bone of the forearm

12. Each shoulder consists of one _____ and one _____.
13. The thorax protects the _____, _____, and other internal organs.
14. Identify the bones of the arm in the corresponding spaces.

   a) _____
   b) _____
   c) _____
   d) _____

Rapid Review Test

Date: _____

Rating: _____

Insert the correct term in the space provided.

hyoid bone	lacrimal bones	radius
cervical vertebrae	lower jawbone	sternum
cheekbones	maxillary	

1. The bones of the upper jaw are the _____.
2. The mandible forms the _____.
3. The eye sockets are formed by small, thin bones called the _____.
4. The two zygomatic or malar bones form the _____.
5. The _____ provides a stable base for tongue movement.

6. Part of the thorax is the _____ or breastbone.
7. The smaller forearm bone, on the thumb side, is the _____.
8. The uppermost seven bones of the vertebral column, located in the neck area, make up the _____.

TOPIC 3: THE MUSCULAR SYSTEM

1. What are the main functions of the muscular system?
   a) _____
   b) _____
2. The body has over 600 muscles, which account for approximately _____ percent of its weight.
3. What are the three types of muscle tissue?
   a) _____ also called skeletal or voluntary.
   b) _____ also called involuntary, visceral, or smooth.
   c) _____ the muscle that makes up the heart.
4. The _____ is the part of the muscle that does not move.
5. The _____ is the part of the muscle at the more movable attachment to the skeleton.
6. Pressure in massage is usually directed from the _____ to the _____.
7. List seven ways in which muscular tissue can be stimulated.
   a) _____   e) _____
   b) _____   f) _____
   c) _____   g) _____
   d) _____
8. The following muscles are located in the scalp, neck, ear, eyebrow, nose, and mouth. Indicate where each of these muscles is located.
   a) _____: orbicularis oris
   b) _____: orbicularis oculi
   c) _____: frontalis
   d) _____: auricularis anterior
   e) _____: procerus
   f) _____: sternocleidomastoideus
9. Identify the muscles of the head, face, and neck in the corresponding spaces.
   a) _____
   b) _____
   c) _____
   d) _____
   e) _____
   f) _____
   g) _____
   h) _____
   i) _____
   j) _____

k) _____
l) _____
m) _____
n) _____
o) _____
p) _____

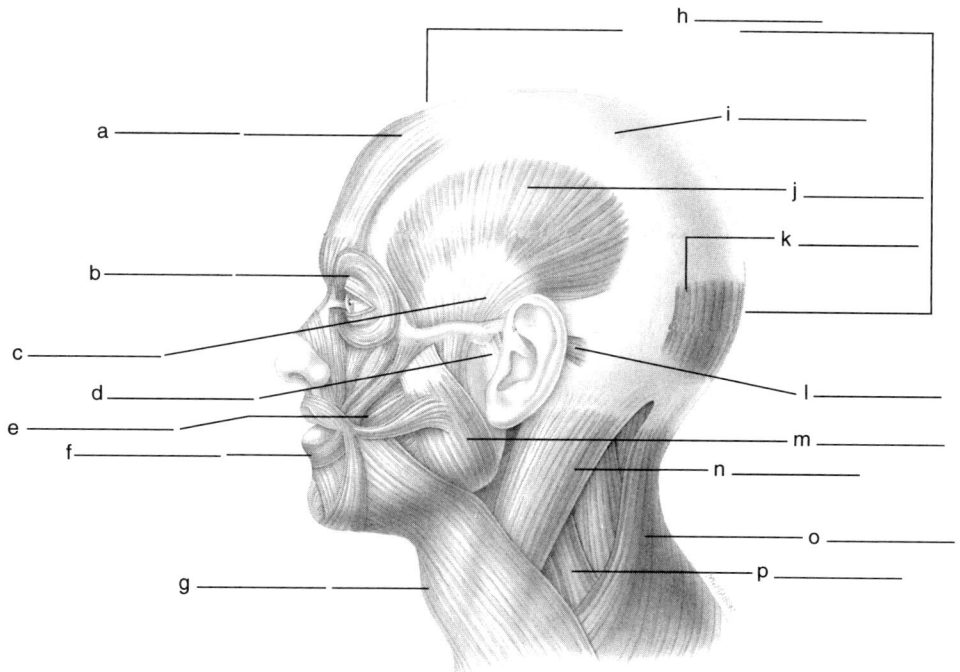

10. The _____ is the broad muscle that covers the top of the skull.
11. The _____ superior, anterior, and posterior are the muscles of the ear.
12. The masseter and temporalis muscles are sometimes referred to as the _____ muscles.
13. The eyebrow muscle that draws the eyebrow down and wrinkles the forehead vertically is the _____ muscle.
14. The _____ covers the bridge of the nose and lowers the eyebrows.
15. Match each of these muscles to its function:

buccinators	levator labii superioris	risorius
depressor labii inferioris	mentalis	triangularis
levator anguli oris	orbicularis oris	zygomaticus major/minor

a) _____ compresses the cheeks and expels air between the lips.
b) _____ draws the corner of the mouth out and back, as in grinning.
c) _____ compresses, contracts, puckers, and wrinkles the lips.
d) _____ raises the angle of the mouth and draws it inward.
e) _____ elevates the lower lip and raises and wrinkles the skin of the chin.
f) _____ depresses the lower lip and draws it to one side.

25

g) _____ elevates the lip, as in laughing.

h) _____ elevates the upper lip and dilates the nostrils, as in expressing distaste.

i) _____ pulls down the corners of the mouth.

16. The broad, flat muscle covering the back of the neck and upper and middle region of the back, controlling the shoulder blade, is called the _____.

17. The _____ is a muscle of the chest that assists in breathing and in raising the arm.

18. Match each of these muscles in the shoulder or arm to its description:

biceps	flexors	supinator	extensors
deltoid	pronators	triceps	

a) _____: wrist muscles involved in bending the wrist

b) _____: muscle producing the contour of the front and inner side of the upper arm

c) _____: muscles that straighten the wrist, hand, and fingers

d) _____: large muscle that covers the entire back of the upper arm and extends the forearm

e) _____: muscle that rotates the radius outward and the palm upward

f) _____: muscles that turn the hand inward so that the palm faces downward

g) _____: large, triangular muscle covering the shoulder joint

19. Identify the muscles of the shoulder and arm in the corresponding spaces.

a) _____

b) _____

c) _____

d) _____

e) _____

f) _____

g) _____

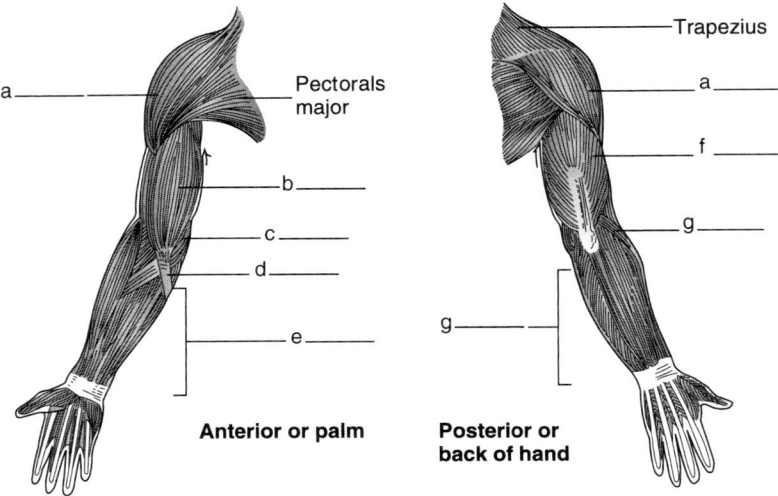

Rapid Review Test

Date: _____

Rating: _____

Insert the correct term in the space provided.

aponeurosis	orbicularis oculi	sternocleidomastoideus
heart	pectoralis	striated
nonstriated	platysma	trapezius
occipitalis		

a) _____ muscles function automatically, without conscious will.

b) Cardiac muscle is found only in the _____.

c) The muscles that are attached to the bones and are controlled by the will are _____ muscles.

d) The back of the epicranius, called the _____, draws the scalp backward.

e) The tendon that connects the occipitalis and frontalis is the _____.

f) The _____ extends from the chest and shoulder muscles to the side of the chin.

g) The _____ lowers and rotates the head.

h) The ring muscle of the eye socket that closes the eye is the _____.

i) The _____ covers the back of the neck and upper and middle regions of the back and helps to shrug the shoulders.

j) The _____ major and minor are muscles of the chest that assist the swinging movements of the arm.

TOPIC 4: THE NERVOUS SYSTEM

1. What is the primary function of the nervous system? _____

2. Name the principal components of the nervous system.

    a) _____

    b) _____

    c) _____

3. What are the two main subdivisions of the nervous system?

    a) _____

    b) _____

4. The spinal cord and brain make up the _____.

5. The _____ nervous system controls the involuntary muscles, such as the glands, blood vessels, and heart.

6. The _____ nervous system carries impulses, or messages, to and from the central nervous system.

7. What is the largest, most complex nerve tissue in the body? _____

8. How many pairs of cranial nerves originate in the brain? _____ How many pairs of spinal nerves extend from the spinal cord? _____

9. Where are the spinal nerves distributed? _____

10. A nerve cell is also called a _____.

11. What is the function of dendrites? _____

12. What is the function of the axon? _____

13. Which type of nerve carries impulses from the brain to the muscles? _____

14. Which type of nerve carries impulses from the sense organs to the brain? _____

15. Pulling the hand away quickly from a hot stove is an example of a _____.

16. The _____ is also known as the trifacial or trigeminal nerve.

17. The three branches of the trifacial or trigeminal nerve are the:

   a) _____

   b) _____

   c) _____

18. Identify the nerves of the head, face, and neck in the corresponding spaces on page 29.

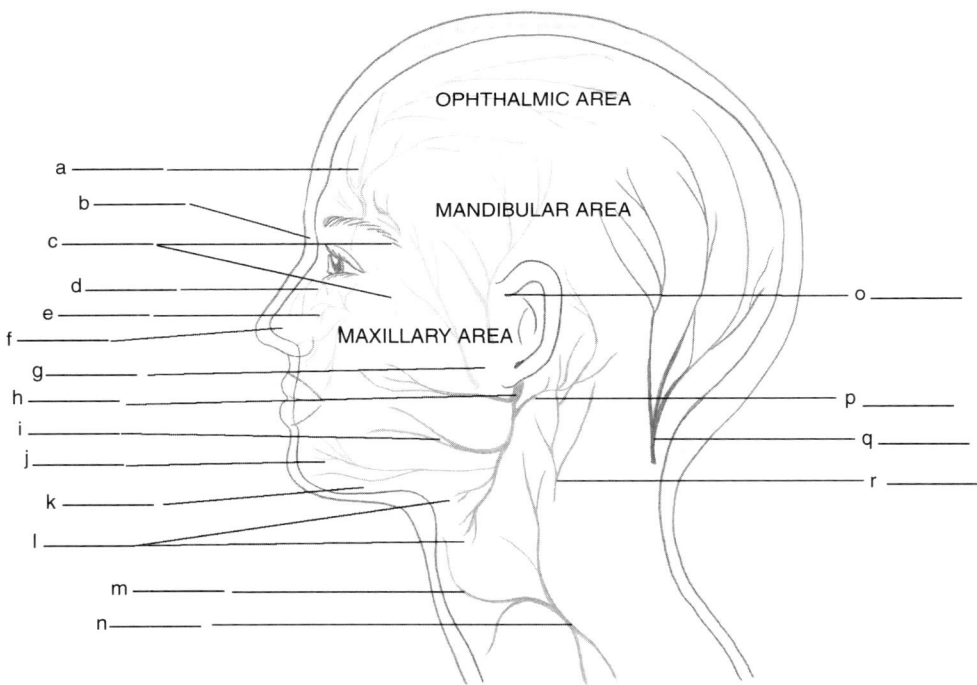

28

a) _____
b) _____
c) _____
d) _____
e) _____
f) _____
g) _____
h) _____
i) _____
j) _____
k) _____
l) _____
m) _____
n) _____
o) _____
p) _____
q) _____
r) _____

19. Match each of the following nerves with its function:

| auriculotemporal | mental | supratrochlear | infratrochlear |
| infraorbital | nasal | zygomatic | supraorbital |

   a) _____ affects the skin of the lower eyelid, side of the nose, upper lip, and mouth.
   b) _____ affects the skin between the eyes and upper side of the nose.
   c) _____ affects the skin of the lower lip and chin.
   d) _____ affects the external ear and skin above the temple, up to the top of the skull.
   e) _____ affects the muscles of the upper part of the cheek.
   f) _____ affects the membrane and skin of the nose.
   g) _____ affects the skin of the forehead, scalp, eyebrow, and upper eyelid.
   h) _____ affects the point and lower side of the nose.

20. The chief motor nerve of the face is the _____ nerve.

21. Match each of the following nerves with its function:

| buccal | posterior auricular | temporal |
| cervical | mandibular | zygomatic |

   a) _____ affects the muscles of the temple, side of the forehead, eyebrow, eyelid, and upper part of the cheek.
   b) _____ affects the side of the neck and the platysma muscle.
   c) _____ affects the muscles of the lower lip and chin.

d) _____ affects the muscles of the mouth.

e) _____ affects the muscles of the upper part of the cheek.

f) _____ affects the muscles behind the ear at the base of the skull.

22. Match each of the following cervical nerves with its function:

cervical cutaneous	greater occipital
greater auricular	smaller occipital

a) _____ affects the scalp and muscles behind the ear.

b) _____ affects the face, ears, neck, and parotid gland.

c) _____ affects the scalp as far up as the top of the head.

d) _____ affects the front and sides of the neck as far down as the breastbone.

23. List the principal nerves of the arm and hand and what parts they supply.

a) _____

b) _____

c) _____

d) _____

TOPIC 5: THE CIRCULATORY SYSTEM

1. What is the primary function of the circulatory system? _____

2. Name the two divisions of the circulatory system and their components:

   a) _____

   b) _____

3. What is the function of lymph? _____

4. What is the function of the heart? _____

5. Identify the parts of the heart in the corresponding spaces on page 31.

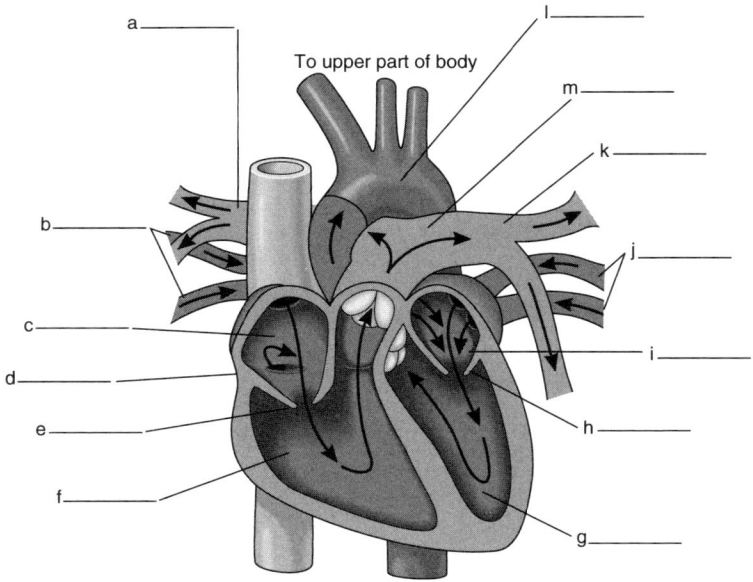

30

a) _____

b) _____

c) _____

d) _____

e) _____

f) _____

g) _____

h) _____

i) _____

j) _____

k) _____

l) _____

m) _____

6. The interior of the heart contains four chambers and _____ valves.

7. When the heart contracts and relaxes, blood flows in and then travels from the _____ to the _____ and out of the heart.

8. What is the normal heartbeat rate in a resting state? _____

9. Name the functions of the following:

   a) pulmonary circulation: _____

   b) systemic circulation: _____

   c) arteries: _____

   d) capillaries: _____

   e) veins: _____

10. Blood has the following characteristics:

    a) There are _____ pints in the human body.

    b) Blood is about _____ percent water.

    c) The normal temperature of blood is _____ Fahrenheit.

    d) Blood is bright red in the _____ and dark red in the _____.

    e) Blood is composed of red and white _____ and _____.

11. Name the five primary functions of blood.

    a) _____

    b) _____
    _____

    c) _____

    d) _____

    e) _____

12. Red blood cells or corpuscles are produced in the _____.

13. Name the functions of these components of blood:

    a) red blood cells: _____

    b) white blood cells: _____

    c) platelets: _____

    d) plasma: _____

14. Lymph is filtered by lymph nodes, a process that helps fight _____.

15. Name the four primary functions of lymph.

   a) _____
   b) _____
   c) _____
   d) _____

16. Identify the arteries of the head, face, and neck in the corresponding spaces.

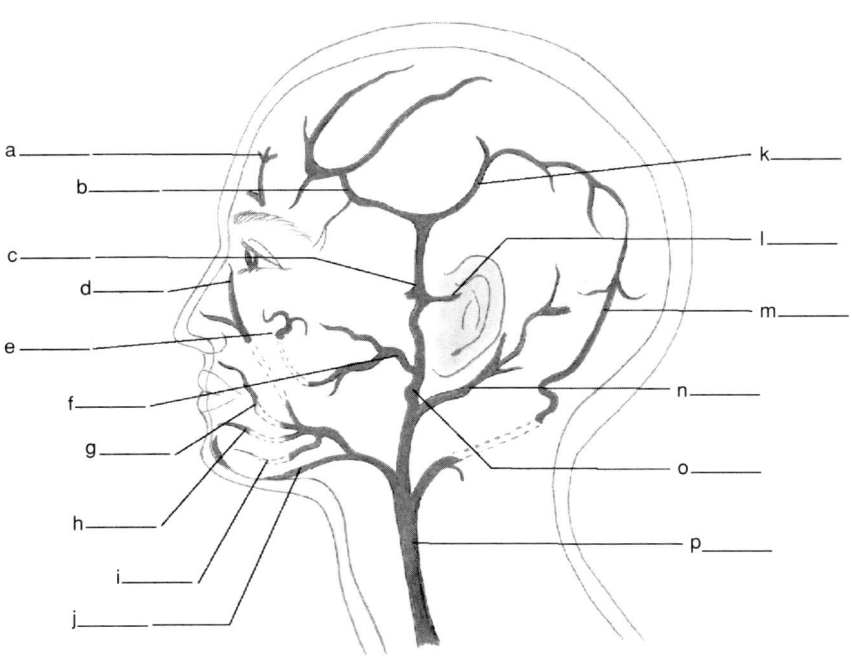

   a) _____
   b) _____
   c) _____
   d) _____
   e) _____
   f) _____
   g) _____
   h) _____
   i) _____
   j) _____
   k) _____
   l) _____
   m) _____
   n) _____
   o) _____
   p) _____

17. The main source of blood supply to the head, face, and neck is the _____ arteries.
18. Match each of the following arteries with the area that it supplies blood to.

angular artery	middle temporal artery	submental artery
anterior auricular artery	occipital artery	superior labial artery
frontal artery	parietal artery	supraorbital artery
inferior labial artery	posterior auricular artery	transverse facial artery
infraorbital artery		

   a) _____: forehead and upper eyelids
   b) _____: scalp, the area behind and above the ear, and the skin behind the ear
   c) _____: upper eyelid and forehead
   d) _____: upper lip and region of the nose
   e) _____: side of the nose
   f) _____: muscles of the eye
   g) _____: temples
   h) _____: chin and lower lip
   i) _____: skin and masseter
   j) _____: front part of the ear
   k) _____: skin and muscles of the scalp and back of the head up to the crown
   l) _____: side and crown of the head
   m) _____: lower lip

19. The two principal veins on each side of the neck are the internal and external _____.
20. _____ are found deep in the tissues, while _____ are closer to the surface of the arms and hands.

Rapid Review Test

Date: _____

Rating: _____

1. Insert the correct term in the space provided.

aorta	leukocytes	ulnar
atrium	pericardium	valve
erythrocytes	platelets	ventricle
hemoglobin	radial	

   a) The heart is enclosed by a membrane called the _____.
   b) The upper, thin-walled chambers of the heart are the right and left _____.
   c) A _____ is one of the lower, thick-walled chambers of the heart.
   d) A _____ is a structure between the chambers of the heart that allows blood to flow in only one direction.
   e) The largest artery in the body is the _____.
   f) Red blood cells are also called red corpuscles or _____.
   g) _____ is the iron protein that gives blood its bright red color.

    h) White blood cells are also called _____.

    i) Thrombocytes are also called _____.

    j) The _____ artery and its branches supply the little-finger side of the arm and palm of the hand.

    k) The _____ artery and its branches supply the thumb side of the arm and the back of the hand.

TOPIC 6: OTHER BODY SYSTEMS

1. The _____ system comprises glands that affect the growth, development, sexual activities, and health of the body.

2. Specialized organs that remove certain elements from the blood and convert them into new compounds are called _____.

3. _____ or duct glands produce a substance that travels through ducts. _____ or ductless glands secrete hormones directly into the bloodstream.

4. Sweat and oil glands are types of _____ glands.

5. Insulin, adrenaline, and estrogen are _____.

6. Digestive _____ are chemicals that change certain kinds of food into a form that can be used by the body.

7. The _____ system purifies the body by eliminating waste matter.

8. What does each of the following organs excrete?

    a) skin: _____

    b) large intestine: _____

    c) kidneys: _____

    d) liver: _____

    e) lungs: _____

9. The respiratory system consists of the _____ and air passages.

10. During inhalation, _____ is absorbed into the blood.

11. During exhalation, the lungs expel _____.

12. The respiratory system is protected on both sides by the _____.

13. The muscular wall that separates the thorax from the abdominal region is the _____.

Date: _____

Rating: _____

Text pages: 127–142

CHAPTER 6
Basics of Chemistry

TOPIC 1: CHEMISTRY

1. Why is it important for estheticians to have a basic knowledge of chemistry?

    a) _____

    b) _____

2. Define chemistry. _____
_____

3. The two branches of chemistry are _____ and _____.

4. Organic chemistry studies substances that contain _____.

5. Gasoline, plastics, synthetic fabrics, pesticides, and fertilizers are manufactured from natural gas and oil and are therefore considered _____.

6. Metals, minerals, pure water, and clean air do not burn and are considered _____.

Rapid Review Test

Date: _____

Rating: _____

Word Review

Match the following terms with their descriptions below.

inorganic	every day	minerals	organic	burn
skin care	chemicals	carbon	reactions	skin care

1. As an esthetician, how often will you be working with chemistry? _____.
2. The daily function of our bodies is based on chemical _____.
3. The skin is made of _____.
4. All _____ products are made of chemicals.
5. _____ substances are not, nor were they ever, alive.
6. _____ are inorganic substances.
7. All living things contain _____.
8. Gasoline and plastics are _____ substances.
9. Organic substances will _____.
10. To understand how _____ products work, estheticians must have a working knowledge of chemistry.

TOPIC 2: MATTER

1. Define matter: _____
2. List the three states of matter, their primary characteristics, and an example of each.
    a) _____
    b) _____
    c) _____
3. What is an element? _____
4. How many naturally occurring elements are there? _____
5. Elements are made up of structural units called _____.
6. Name the smaller particles that make up atoms and indicate the electrical charge of each:
    a) _____
    b) _____
    c) _____
7. Chemically joining two or more atoms creates a _____.
8. Elemental molecules contain two or more atoms of the same element that are united _____.
9. Chemical combinations of two or more atoms of different elements are _____.
10. Define compound. _____
11. What is the most abundant of all elements, comprising about 75 percent of the earth's surface and about 65 percent of the human body? _____
12. Color, weight, melting point, and odor are examples of _____ properties.
13. When wood is burned and turns into ash, there is a change in its _____ properties.
14. Define these terms, and give an example of each:
    a) Physical change: _____
    b) Chemical change: _____
15. Identify the following elements, compounds, or mixtures in the spaces provided:
    a) _____: gaseous mixture that makes up the earth's atmosphere
    b) _____: most abundant element found both free and in compounds
    c) _____: colorless liquid that is a compound of hydrogen and oxygen
    d) _____: gaseous element that comprises about four-fifths of the air
    e) _____: most abundant of all substances, comprising about 75 percent of the earth's surface
    f) _____: lightest element known; flammable and explosive when mixed with air
16. Oxygen combines with many other elements to form compounds called _____.
17. _____ is found mostly in the form of ammonia and nitrates.
18. One of the important chemical characteristics of oxygen is its ability to support _____.
19. The most commonly used ingredient in cosmetics is _____.
20. A 10-percent volume solution of _____ has antiseptic properties.

Rapid Review Test

Date: _____

Rating: _____

Word Review

neutron	energy	molecule	atoms	gas
negative	matter	element	solid	solids
proton	electron	electrons	liquid	chemical
hydrogen	nitrogen	oxygen	water	solution

Match the following terms with their descriptions below.

molecules	liquid	gaseous	elemental	chemical
solid	gas	molecule	reaction	oxygen
temperature	physical	hydrogen	water	nitrogen

1. There are three states of matter: _____.
2. _____ are also called compounds.
3. Oxygen is a(n) _____ molecule.
4. When all the atoms that form a molecule are the same, the molecule is called an _____ molecule.
5. The difference in states of matter depends on _____.
6. Steam is _____ water.
7. Every substance has unique _____ and _____ properties.
8. Chemical properties are those characteristics that can be determined only with a chemical _____.
9. _____ is the lightest element known.
10. _____ is the most abundant of all substances.
11. Hydrogen peroxide is a chemical compound of hydrogen and _____.
12. _____ makes up four-fifths of the air in our atmosphere.

TOPIC 3: POTENTIAL HYDROGEN (pH)

1. What is pH? _____
   _____
2. Name the characteristics of acids and alkalis/bases:

   a) acids: _____
   _____

   b) alkalis or bases _____
   _____

3. What is the neutral pH of skin? _____
4. A pH of 6 is _____ times more alkaline than a pH of 5 and _____ times more alkaline than a pH of 4.
5. What are the functions of the acid mantle? _____
   _____
   _____
6. What is the average pH of the acid mantle? _____
7. _____ may result if the skin is exposed to a low or high pH.

Rapid Review Test

Date: _____

Rating: _____

True or False

1. _____ A natural pH of the skin is 7.0.

2. _____ Alkalies or bases have a pH above 7.0.

3. _____ A pH of 9.0 is 100 times more alkaline than a pH of 8.0.

4. _____ When the pH of the skin is raised or lowered, inflammation can occur.

TOPIC 4: CHEMICAL REACTIONS

1. Define the following terms:
   a) oxidation: _____
   b) reduction: _____
   c) combustion: _____
   _____
   d) redox: _____
   _____

2. An oxidizing agent releases _____.
3. When oxygen is removed from a substance, it is _____.
4. _____ (redox) reactions are one of the most common types of chemical reactions.
5. An oxidation reaction is a _____ from the oxidizer to the substance that is oxidized.
6. Oxidation cannot happen without _____.
7. _____ prevent oxidation by neutralizing free radicals.
8. Oxidation and _____ always occur at the same time.

Rapid Review Test

Date: _____

Rating: _____

Word Review

oxidation	oxidizer	reduction	antioxidant	reduce
redox	oxygen	neutralize	combustion	fire

Match the following terms with their descriptions below.

antioxidants	base	redox	heat
light	free radical	acid–alkali	DNA

1. _____ are highly reactive.
2. One _____ can oxidize millions of other substances.
3. _____ reactions cause iron to rust.
4. _____ neutralization reactions occur when an acid is mixed with an alkali.
5. An alkali is also called a(n) _____.
6. Combustion is the rapid oxidation of a substance, accompanied by the production of _____ and _____.
7. Free radicals have the ability to damage the _____.

TOPIC 5: CHEMISTRY AS APPLIED TO COSMETICS

1. Solutions, suspensions, and emulsions are all kinds of _____.
2. Identify the following substances in the spaces provided:
   a) _____: substance that dissolves another substance to form a solution
   b) _____: uniform mixture of two or more substances
   c) _____: uniform mixture of two or more mutually mixable substances
   d) _____: suspensions (mixtures) of an unstable mixture of two or more immiscible substances united with the aid of an emulsifier
   e) _____: any substance that is dissolved by a solvent to form a solution
   f) _____: liquids that are mutually soluble
3. Define *immiscible liquids*, and give an example. _____
4. List three characteristics of solutions:
   a) _____
   b) _____
   c) _____
5. List three characteristics of suspensions:
   a) _____
   b) _____
   c) _____
6. What does the term *emulsify* mean? _____
7. What are the substances that allow oil and water to mix? _____
8. Name and describe the two parts of a surfactant molecule.
   a) _____
   b) _____

9. List and define the two types of emulsions used in cosmetics.

   a) _____

   b) _____

10. O/W emulsions usually contain more _____ than _____.

11. What is one advantage of O/W emulsions? _____

12. Give examples of O/W emulsions. _____

13. Give examples of W/O emulsions. _____
    _____

14. If a cosmetic emulsion product separates, it should be _____.

Rapid Review Test

Date: _____

Rating: _____

Word Review

suspension	miscible	solution	mixture	unstable
surfactant	emulsion	lipophilic	oil-in-water	solvent

Match the following terms with their descriptions below.

oil-in-water	solute	uniform	emulsions	greasier
heavier	lipophilic	water-in-oil	micelles	saponification
surfactants	solutions	suntan	suspensions	milky

1. Solutions are _____ mixtures of two or more mutually mixable substances.

2. A _____ is any substance that is dissolved by a solvent to form a solution.

3. In _____ solutions, droplets of oil are dispersed in water.

4. In _____ solutions, droplets of water are dispersed in oil.

5. W/O emulsions are _____, _____, and more water-resistant than O/W emulsions.

6. In O/W emulsions, droplets of oil or _____ are surrounded by surfactants with their tails or _____ ends pointing in.

7. Modern soaps are made by a process called _____.

8. O/W emulsions are often _____, free-flowing liquids.

9. O/W emulsions including moisturizing lotions, cleansing lotions, and _____ lotions.

10. _____ differ from solutions due to the size of the particles.

11. _____, suspensions, and emulsions are all physical mixtures of two or more different substances.

12. _____ are used to emulsify oil-and-water to create an emulsion.

True or False

1. _____ A surfactant molecule has two distinct parts that make the emulsification of oil and water possible.

2. _____ Oil-in-water emulsions usually contain a small amount of oil and a greater amount of water.

3. _____ Miscible liquids are mutually insoluble.

4. _____ Oil-and-vinegar salad dressing is an example of a miscible solution.

5. _____ In oil-in-water emulsions, the water phase protects the surface of the epidermis.

6. _____ Most lotions and creams used by estheticians are oil-in-water emulsions.

7. _____ Paint and aerosol hair spray are examples of emulsions.

Date: _____

Rating: _____

Text pages: 143–161

CHAPTER 7
Basics of Electricity

TOPIC 1: BASICS OF ELECTRICITY

1. Define electricity. _____
   _____

2. Electricity is a flow of _____ that are negatively charged particles swirling around atoms like a swarm of bees.

3. Any substance that easily transmits electricity is called a _____.

4. A substance that does not easily transmit electricity is called a nonconductor or _____.

5. In electric wires, the twisted metal threads are the _____, and the rubber or silk that covers them are the _____.

6. What is the difference between direct and alternating current? _____
   _____
   _____

7. What is the difference between a converter and a rectifier? _____
   _____

8. What do the following electrical units measure?
   a) volt: _____
   b) ohm: _____
   c) amp: _____
   d) watt: _____

9. One-thousandth of an ampere is a _____.

10. One thousand watts is a _____.

11. Identify the device that performs the following functions:
    a) _____: completes the circuit and carries the current safely away to the ground.
    b) _____: prong connector at the end of an electrical cord that connects an apparatus to an electrical outlet
    c) _____: device that blows out or melts when the wire becomes too hot from overloading the circuit with too much current
    d) _____: plug-in device used to make electrical contact
    e) _____: switch that automatically interrupts or shuts off an electric circuit at the first indication of overload

12. The UL symbol on an electrical appliance, which stands for _____, certifies the safety of the appliance.

13. Electrical plugs with one prong that is slightly larger than the other can be inserted only one way and protect you from _____ in case of a short circuit.

14. Fill in the missing terms in the following precautions:
    a) When appliances are not being used, they should be _____.
    b) Use _____ plug(s) per outlet.
    c) Avoid contact with _____ and metal surfaces when you are using electricity.
    d) Disconnect appliances by pulling on the _____.
    e) Allowing an electrical cord to become twisted may cause a _____.
    f) Do not clean around electric outlets while equipment is _____.
    g) Do not leave any client _____ while connected to an electrical device.

Rapid Review Test

Date: _____

Rating: _____

Word Review

Insert the correct term in the space provided.

insulators	conductor	amp
circuit breakers	ground	watts
complete circuit		

1. Copper is an especially good _____.
2. A _____ is the path of an electric current from the generating source back to its original source.
3. Rubber, silk, cement, wood, and glass are good _____.
4. A higher _____ reading indicates a stronger electrical current.
5. A 60-watt light bulb uses 60 _____ of energy per second.
6. _____ have largely replaced fuses in modern electric circuits.
7. A third, circular prong on an electric plug provides additional _____.

TOPIC 2: ELECTROTHERAPY

1. The term for electronic facial treatments is _____.
2. The various currents used in facial and scalp treatments are called _____.
3. What is polarity? _____
4. Name and briefly describe the two poles of an electric current.
    a) _____
    b) _____
5. What are the four modalities used in cosmetology?
    a) _____
    b) _____
    c) _____
    d) _____
6. Describe galvanic current. _____

7. List the effects of the positive and negative poles of the galvanic current.

   Positive Pole (Anode)   **Negative Pole (Cathode)**

   _____   _____
   _____   _____
   _____   _____
   _____   _____
   _____   _____
   _____   _____
   _____   _____

8. Negative galvanic current should not be used on clients with:

   a) _____

   b) _____

   c) _____

   d) _____

9. Match the following terms with their descriptions below.

   | anaphoresis | desincrustation |
   | cataphoresis | iontophoresis |

   a) _____: process used to soften and emulsify grease deposits and blackheads in the hair follicles

   b) _____: process that forces acidic substances into deeper tissues from the positive toward the negative pole

   c) _____: process that introduces water-soluble products into the skin with electric current, such as the positive and negative poles of a galvanic machine

   d) _____: process that forces liquids into tissues from the negative toward the positive pole

10. What is a faradic current, and how is it used? _____
    _____

11. What are the benefits of using faradic current in a facial treatment?

    a) _____
    b) _____
    c) _____
    d) _____
    e) _____
    f) _____
    g) _____

12. Sinusoidal current is similar to _____ current, but it is less irritating.

13. _____ mimics the way that the brain relays messages to the muscles.

14. The Tesla high-frequency current is a _____ current that requires only one _____.

15. The benefits of the Tesla high-frequency current in skin treatments are:

    a) _____
    b) _____

c) _____
d) _____
e) _____
f) _____

16. What are the two methods used to apply Tesla high-frequency current?
    a) _____
    b) _____

17. In which method of Tesla high-frequency current application does the client hold the electrode? _____

18. How can you prevent sparking when handling an electrode? _____

19. A client being treated with Tesla high-frequency current should avoid any contact with _____.

20. What kind of skin is particularly suited for indirect high-frequency current application? _____

Rapid Review Test

Date: _____

Rating: _____

Word Review

Insert the correct term in the space provided.

| active | modalities | Tesla high-frequency |
| desincrustation | electrode | polarity |

1. _____ indicates the negative or positive pole of an electric current.
2. Galvanic and high-frequency currents are examples of _____.
3. In a treatment with galvanic current, the _____ electrode is the one used on the area to be treated.
4. A process using galvanic current that is used to treat acne, milia, and comedones is called _____.
5. The _____ current is commonly called the violet ray.
6. In the direct surface application of high-frequency current, apply the _____ to specific areas for healing acne and disinfecting the skin.

TOPIC 3: LIGHT THERAPY

1. Define light therapy. _____
2. _____ is electromagnetic radiation that we can see.
3. A _____ is the distance between the peaks of two successive waves of electromagnetic radiation.
4. Shorter wavelengths have a higher _____ than longer wavelengths.
5. Visible light makes up _____ percent of natural sunlight.
6. Ultraviolet rays and infrared rays are _____ forms of electromagnetic radiation.
7. Among the visible light rays, _____ has the shortest wavelength and _____ has the longest.

8. Ultraviolet (UV) rays—also called actinic rays—make up _____ percent of natural sunlight.

9. _____ rays cause damage to collagen and fibrils.

10. When compared to visible light, UV rays:

    a) _____

    b) _____

    c) _____

11. _____ are also called the burning rays.

12. Natural sunlight produces vitamin _____ in the skin.

13. UV rays stimulate the production of _____ in the skin.

14. How many new cases of skin cancer are diagnosed each year? _____ What percentage of cancer cases is caused by overexposure to UV radiation? _____

15. Infrared rays are used in spas and saunas for _____.

16. _____ rays make up 60 percent of natural sunlight.

17. When compared to visible light, infrared rays:

    a) _____

    b) _____

    c) _____

18. White light is referred to as _____ because it is a combination of all the visible rays of the spectrum.

19. _____ light contains few heat rays, is the least penetrating, and has some germicidal and chemical benefits.

20. _____ light is used on dry skin in combination with oils and creams. It produces the most _____ and penetrates the _____.

21. List the beneficial effects of the following forms of light therapy.

    Ultraviolet light:

    a) _____

    b) _____

    c) _____

    d) _____

    e) _____

    Infrared light:

    a) _____

    b) _____

    c) _____

    d) _____

    e) _____

    f) _____

    g) _____

    White light:

    a) _____

    b) _____

    c) _____

Blue light:

a) _____

b) _____

c) _____

d) _____

e) _____

f) _____

Red light:

a) _____

b) _____

c) _____

d) _____

e) _____

22. Laser is an acronym for _____.

23. Which device uses multiple colors of focused light to treat spider veins and brown spots? _____ _____

24. _____ devices release a flashing light on the skin that, in turn, releases healing enzymes in the skin that cause healing.

Rapid Review Test

Date: _____

Rating: _____

Word Review

Insert the correct term in the space provided.

blue light	infrared lamps	UVC rays
UV rays	laser	red light

1. _____ devices work by selective photothermolysis.
2. _____ soothes nerves, improves acne, and provides some chemical and germicidal effects.
3. _____ is used to treat aging skin.
4. _____ are often used in salons for heating conditioners and chemicals in hair treatments.
5. _____ have germicidal qualities and, in larger amounts, will eliminate life as we know it.
6. _____ can produce painful burns and blistering, increase the risk of skin cancer, and cause premature aging.

Date: _____

Rating: _____

Text pages: 162–186

CHAPTER 8
Basics of Nutrition

TOPIC 1: BASICS OF NUTRITION

1. _____ needs depend on a variety of factors such as age, sex, weight, physical activity, and body type.
2. The _____ is the governmental department that regulates nutrition-related affairs.
3. _____ or _____ can affect the ability to digest food and interrupt the normal process of nutrients reaching the bloodstream and, consequently, the cells.
4. _____ begins with a good diet and water intake.
5. Skin disorders, fatigue, stress, depression, and some diseases are often the result of a _____.
6. _____ make up the largest part of the nutrition we take in.
7. Macronutrients are the three basic food groups: _____.
8. Proteins are chains of _____ molecules used by every cell of the body to make other usable proteins.
9. Proteins contain all essential _____.
10. Plant sources are not _____, because they all lack at least one of the essential amino acids.
11. _____ are combinations of two incomplete proteins that provide all the essential amino acids and make a complete protein.
12. Dietary sources of protein come from _____.
13. _____ are also called complex carbohydrates.
14. The three basic types of carbohydrates are _____.
15. Saturated fats come mainly from _____.
16. Obesity is determined by a BMI of _____ or greater.
17. _____ assist in the absorption of the fat-soluble vitamins A, D, E, and K.
18. _____ are the main fats in foods.
19. Starches are present in many _____.
20. Dietitians generally believe that _____ percent of all calories should be obtained from carbohydrates.
21. Protein requirements range from _____ percent.
22. _____ are biological catalysts made of protein and vitamins.
23. _____ are carbohydrate-lipid complexes that are good water binders.
24. _____ or lipids are macronutrients.

25. _____ can increase the bad type of cholesterol in the blood known as LDL or _____.

26. _____ are a good type of cholesterol in the blood.

Rapid Review Test

Date: _____

Rating: _____

Word Review

| trans fatty acids | enzymes | HDLs | LDLs | macronutrients | proteins |
| micronutrients | fats | triglycerides | BMI | lipids | obesity |

Match the following terms with their descriptions below.

carbohydrates	glucose	fats
monosaccharides	mucopolysaccharides	polysaccharides
calories	starches	fiber
enzymes	omega-3	simple sugars

1. _____ break down the basic chemical sugars that supply energy for the body.
2. _____ is stored in the muscles and liver as glycogen.
3. _____ are present in the dermis as glycosaminoglycans.
4. _____ are the simplest of all carbohydrates.
5. _____ include sucrose, fructose, and lactose.
6. _____ include starch and fiber.
7. _____ is necessary for proper digestion.
8. _____ include cereals, breads, other flour products, potatoes, rice, and pasta.
9. _____ reduce materials in the body into carbon dioxide, water, and unnecessary end products that are excreted.
10. _____ are used to produce the materials in the sebaceous glands that lubricate the skin.
11. _____ is a type of good fat.
12. _____ are a measure of heat units.

TOPIC 2: MICRONUTRIENTS

1. _____ are also called micronutrients.
2. Ideally, the nutrients the body needs for proper functioning and survival should come primarily from the _____.
3. Fat-soluble vitamins A, D, E, and K are generally present in _____ within foods.
4. Vitamins fall into two categories: _____.
5. _____ is necessary for proper eyesight.
6. Vitamin A is a group of compounds called _____.
7. _____ is sometimes called the sunshine vitamin.

49

8. The main function of vitamin D is to enable the body to _____.
9. Vitamin E or _____ is primarily an antioxidant.
10. _____ is essential for the synthesis of proteins necessary for blood coagulation.
11. Water-soluble vitamins _____ benefit the inside of cells.
12. List the eight B vitamins:

   a) _____
   b) _____
   c) _____
   d) _____
   e) _____
   f) _____
   g) _____
   h) _____

13. Riboflavin or _____ is a water-soluble vitamin that works with enzymes to produce energy in cells.
14. Niacin is required for the manufacture of _____ by the body as well as for the manufacture of _____.
15. Thiamine or _____ removes carbon dioxide from cells and converts carbohydrates stored as _____.
16. Folacin is also known as _____.
17. _____ is involved in energy formation by cells as well as in the synthesis of both proteins and fatty acids.
18. Vitamin C or _____ is an antioxidant that helps protect the body from many forms of oxidation and free-radical-induced problems.
19. Liver, salmon, clams, oysters, and egg yolks are good food sources of _____.
20. A vitamin C deficiency can cause a disease called _____.
21. _____ are inorganic materials required for many reactions of the cells and the body.
22. Bioflavonoids are referred to as _____.
23. _____ moves carbon dioxide and regulates water levels and the transport of materials through the cell membranes.
24. Iron, iodine, zinc, copper, chromium, fluoride, selenium, and manganese are all _____.
25. Walking burns _____ calories per hour.
26. Running burns _____ calories per hour.

Rapid Review Test

Date: _____

Rating: _____

Word Review

minerals	chromium	ascorbic acid	sodium
vitamin B	steroids	fluoride	scurvy

Match the following terms with their descriptions below.

chromium	vitamin B₁₂	water-soluble	osteomalacia
rickets	niacin	minerals	fat-soluble

1. _____ helps with energy and the metabolism of glucose; aids in the synthesis of fats and proteins.
2. _____ is a deficiency disease due to lack of vitamin D.
3. _____ are inorganic materials required for many reactions of the cells and the body.
4. _____ is important in the activation of folacin, fatty acid synthesis, and DNA synthesis.
5. _____ vitamins are used in almost every metabolic reaction and are then excreted.
6. _____ is the adult form of rickets.
7. _____ vitamins are stored in the body.
8. _____ deficiencies can cause pellagra, a disease that affects the skin, mental functions, intestinal tract, and may even cause death.

TOPIC 3: NUTRITION AND ESTHETICS

1. Excess _____ may trigger acne.
2. All clients who have serious questions about nutritional issues should be referred to a _____.
3. The only way to lose weight is to _____ than you consume.
4. Vitamins and mineral supplements are not substitutes for _____.
5. _____ are grown without pesticides and added chemicals.
6. Water composes _____ percent of the body's weight.
7. _____ aids in proper digestion, elimination of toxins and waste, and regulation of the body's temperature.
8. The amount of water needed by an individual varies, depending on _____.

Rapid Review Test

Date: _____

Rating: _____

Word Review

Match the following terms with their descriptions below.

organic foods	chemical imbalances	hormonal imbalances
registered dietician	rosacea	water

1. _____ can be caused by certain diets that are harmful to the body.
2. A 2 percent drop in _____ can trigger fuzzy short-term memory, trouble with basic math, and difficulty focusing on a computer screen or printed page.
3. _____ flare-ups can be triggered by spicy foods and alcohol consumption.
4. _____ can be the result of extremely low body fat.
5. _____ do not use synthetic fertilizers.
6. A _____ has a degree in nutrition.

Date: _____

Rating: _____

Text pages: 187–209

CHAPTER 9

Physiology and Histology of the Skin

INTRODUCTION
1. _____ is the study of the structure and composition of skin tissue.
2. _____ is the study of the functions of living organisms.
3. An esthetician's primary focus is _____ the skin.

TOPIC 1: STRUCTURE AND FUNCTION OF THE SKIN
1. The skin is the primary component of which body system? _____
2. Identify four healthy skin characteristics.
    a) _____   c) _____
    b) _____   d) _____
3. On which parts of the body is skin the thickest and the thinnest? _____
   _____
4. List the six primary functions of the skin.
    a) _____   d) _____
    b) _____   e) _____
    c) _____   f) _____
5. What substance helps to lubricate and protect the skin? _____
6. In every square inch of skin there are millions of _____, 65 _____, 1,300 _____, and 15 feet of _____.
7. The skin is a protective barrier to _____.
8. The _____ is the protective barrier of the skin.
9. The acid mantle is part of the skin's natural _____.
10. Water loss due to evaporation on the skin's surface is called _____ or _____.
11. The skin's most amazing ability is to _____.
12. _____ cells are guard cells.
13. Our _____ kicks in when guard cells sense unrecognized foreign invaders.
14. _____ is the pigment that protects us from the sun.
15. _____ in the dermis respond to touch, pain, cold, heat, and pressure.
16. When the outside temperature changes, the skin adjusts to _____ the body.
17. The _____ or _____ glands excrete perspiration and detoxify the body.
18. The oils secreted by the _____ keep the skin soft and protect it from outside elements.
19. The skin absorbs _____ and discharges _____.
20. The skin is composed of two parts: _____.

21. The _____ is the outermost layer of the skin.
22. _____ and epithelial cells protect the epidermis.
23. The epidermis is composed of five layers called _____. Starting with the top layer, they are:
    a) _____
    b) _____
    c) _____
    d) _____
    e) _____
24. Estheticians are licensed to work only on the _____.
25. The _____ is the outermost layer of the epidermis.
26. Keratin is a fiber _____ that provides _____ and _____ to the skin.
27. _____ are intercellular connections that provide strength to the cells.
28. The process of shedding old cells that are continually replaced by new ones is called _____.
29. The _____ is a clear layer under the stratum corneum.
30. The _____ is composed of cells that resemble granules.
31. The _____ is a spiny layer above the basal layer.
32. The _____ is also known as the basal layer of the epidermis.
33. The _____ is the live layer of connective tissues below the epidermis.
34. The dermis consists of two layers: _____.
35. The _____ layer connects the dermis to the epidermis.
36. The _____ layer is the deeper layer of the dermis.
37. Cell division is called _____.
38. As cells divide, they migrate to the _____ and become _____.
39. Collagen is produced by _____.
40. _____ is a protein substance that gives skin its strength and is necessary for wound healing.
41. In the dermis, there is a fluid matrix called _____.
42. Below the reticular layer, there is a subcutaneous layer called _____ tissue.
43. Hair contains _____.
44. Hair—a slender, threadlike outgrowth—is an _____ of the skin.
45. _____ is the technical name for the nail.
46. List the classifications of nerves and their functions:
    a) _____
    b) _____
    c) _____
       _____
47. _____ are cells that produce pigment granules in the basal layer. These granules are called _____.
48. _____ determines skin and hair color.
49. The body produces two types of melanin: _____.
50. The excretion of sweat is controlled by the _____.
51. Normally _____ pints of liquids containing salts are eliminated daily through sweat pores in the skin.
52. The _____ are coiled structures attached to the hair follicles found under the arms and in the genital area.
53. The _____ are found all over the body, but primarily on the forehead, palms, and soles.

53

Rapid Review Test

Date: _____

Rating: _____

Word Review

Match the following terms with their descriptions below.

stratum corneum	melanin	arrector pili
dermis	adipose	elastin
epidermis	collagen	hyaluronic acid
keratin	sebaceous	tactile

1. _____: refers to the substance that keeps skin soft and protected
2. _____: deeper layer of the skin
3. _____: fiber protein that provides resiliency and protection to the skin
4. _____: top layer of the skin
5. _____: outermost layer of the skin
6. _____: skin pigment
7. _____: muscles that cause goose bumps
8. _____: a glycosaminoglycan (GAG) that hydrates the skin
9. _____: sense of touch
10. _____: subcutaneous layer composed of fat
11. _____: makes up 70 percent of the dermis
12. _____: fibrous protein that forms elastic tissue and gives skin its elasticity

From the following list of parts of the skin, identify the numbered parts on the illustration. Insert the proper term in the space provided.

Adipose (fatty) tissue	Mouth of follicle	Stratum lucidum
Arrector pili muscle	Papillary layer of dermis	Stratum spinosum
Arteries	Reticular layer of dermis	Subcutaneous tissue
Dermal papilla	Sebaceous (oil) gland	Sudoriferous gland
Dermis (true skin)	Stratum corneum	Sweat pore
Epidermis	Stratum germinativum (Basal layer)	Veins
Hair shaft	Stratum granulosum	

1. _____
2. _____
3. _____
4. _____
5. _____
6. _____
7. _____
8. _____
9. _____
10 _____
11. _____
12. _____
13. _____
14. _____
15. _____
16. _____
17. _____
18. _____
19. _____
20. _____

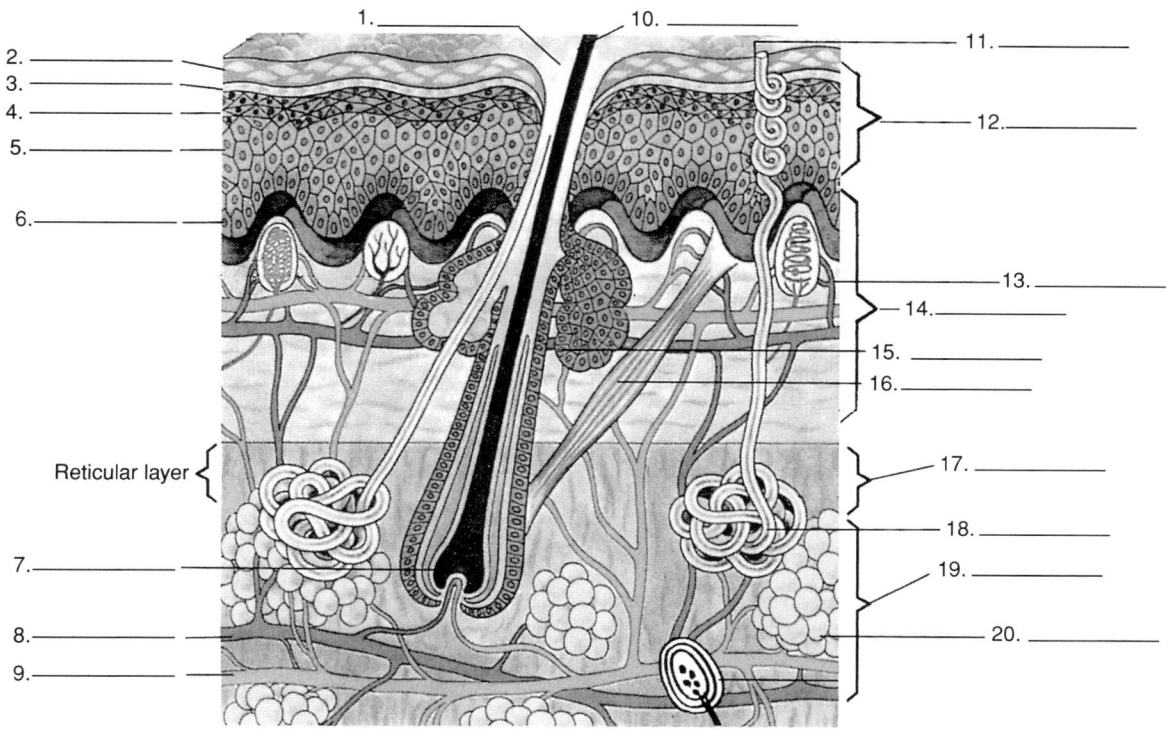

Reticular layer

TOPIC 2: SKIN HEALTH

1. _____ and _____ are both influenced by many different factors, including heredity, sun exposure, the environment, health habits, and general lifestyle.

2. Which fluids nourish the skin? _____

3. Networks of _____ and _____ send essential materials for growth and repair throughout the body.

4. _____ bathes the skin cells, removes toxins and cellular waste, and has immune functions that help protect the skin and body against disease.

5. Cells need these important elements to survive:

   a) _____

   b) _____

   c) _____

   d) _____

6. The health of the skin depends on the cellular membrane and the _____ _____.

7. Phospholipids, glycolipids, cholesterol, triglycerides, squalene, and waxes are all _____.

8. _____ and _____ surround cells and provide protection, hydration, and nourishment to the cells.

9. Cell recovery depends on _____ to recover properly.

10. _____ and _____ are not easily replaced by the body, and the skin does not regain its once pliable shape after being stretched or damaged by _____.

11. _____ are atoms or molecules with unpaired electrons.

12. Photodamage causes _____.

13. Red and inflamed skin are signs of _____.

14. The best defense against damaging pollutants is to follow a _____.

15. The impact of poor lifestyle choices can be seen most visibly _____.

55

16. Heavy or excessive intake of alcohol dilates the _____.
17. _____ have the greatest impact on how skin ages.
18. The two types of rays that reach the skin are _____.
19. _____, also called the aging rays, contribute to (90 to 95) percent of the sun's ultraviolet rays that reach the earth's surface.
20. _____, also referred to as the burning rays, cause the skin to burn.
21. UVA and UVB rays alter _____ and can cause skin cancer.
22. _____ contribute to the synthesis of vitamin D.
23. All sunscreen used for protection should be broad spectrum to filter out _____.
24. Many topical products and medications are _____ that can cause severe skin reactions, such as burning.
25. _____ is the hormone that is key to the good health and appearance of skin.
26. Estrogen is _____, _____, and a key factor in _____.
27. As the skin matures, collagen loses its ability to respond to physical changes from _____.
28. _____ is the term used for dilation of the capillary walls.
29. _____ is a chronic disorder characterized by couperose veins and congestion of the skin.
30. Hormone replacement therapies can be derived from _____ or _____ source estrogens.

Rapid Review Test

Date: _____

Rating: _____

Word Review

| estrogen | anti-inflammatory | free radical | photosensitizer | tissue repair |
| telangiectasia | intercellular lipids | photoaging | antioxidant | DNA |

Match the following terms with their descriptions below.

| lymph | vitamin D | smoking | UV rays | rosacea | phytoestrogens |
| bones | estrogen | free radicals | nutrients | cell damage | blood |

1. _____: cumulative
2. _____: replaced every seven years
3. _____: super oxidizers
4. _____: fluids that nourish the skin
5. _____: have the greatest impact on skin aging
6. _____: synthesized by UVB rays
7. _____: hormone that is key to the good health and appearance of skin
8. _____: ages the skin
9. _____: derived from the three basic food groups (carbohydrates, proteins, and fats)
10. _____: supplies nutrients and oxygen to the skin
11. _____: can foster parasitic organisms (mites)
12. _____: Mexican wild yam, sage, hops, soy

Date: _____

Rating: _____

Text pages: 210–233

CHAPTER 10

Disorders and Diseases of the Skin

TOPIC 1: DERMATOLOGY AND ESTHETICS

1. The esthetician should be able to identify skin disorders that may be treated in the salon and those that require _____.

2. _____ is the branch of medical science that studies and treats the skin and its disorders and diseases.

TOPIC 2: LESIONS

1. _____ are structural changes in the tissues caused by damage or injury.

2. Name the characteristic primary lesion present in each of the following conditions.

   a) _____: discolored spot or patch that is neither raised nor sunken

   b) _____: small, fluidless elevation of the skin

   c) _____: itchy, swollen lesion

   d) _____: abnormal solid lump larger than a papule

   e) _____: external swelling from excessive cell multiplication that varies in shape and color

   f) _____: blister with clear fluid inside

   g) _____: large blister containing a watery fluid similar to a vesicle

   h) _____: elevation of the skin that is inflamed and contains pus

   i) _____: small bumps caused by scar tissue, fatty deposits, or infections

   j) _____: closed, abnormally developed sac containing fluid, infection, or other matter above or below the skin

3. Name the characteristic secondary lesion that develops in the later stages of a disease.

   a) _____: accumulation of epidermal flakes, dry or oily

   b) _____: accumulation of sebum and pus mixed with other epidermal waste

   c) _____: skin sore or abrasion caused by scratching or scraping the skin

   d) _____: crack in the skin that may penetrates the dermis

   e) _____: open lesion on the skin or mucous membrane of the body, accompanied by pus and loss of skin depth

   f) _____: likely to form after the healing of a skin injury or condition

   g) _____: scraping off of acne lesions, causing scarring and discoloration

   h) _____: thick scar resulting from excessive growth of fibrous tissue

Rapid Review Test

Date _____

Rating _____

Word Review

Match the following terms with their descriptions below.

abrasion	scale	ulcer
crust	ulcer	wheal
dermatology	tertiary	tumors
keloid		

1. A scab is another name for a _____.
2. The study of _____ deals with diseases of the skin.
3. A thick scar resulting from excessive growth of tissue is called a _____.
4. An epidermal flake is the same as a _____.
5. An open lesion of the skin or mucous membrane with loss of skin depth is an _____.
6. An insect bite causes a lesion known as a _____.
7. Nodules are referred to as _____.
8. There are three types of lesions: primary, secondary, and _____.
9. Another name for excoriation is _____.
10. An open lesion accompanied by pus and loss of skin depth is called a(n) _____.

RAPID REVIEW TEST

Date: _____

Rating: _____

Insert the proper term in the space provided for the following definitions with the illustration that it correctly describes.

A(n) _____ is rough and red where the skin has been scraped or worn away.

A(n) _____ is an open lesion on the skin or mucous membrane of the body, accompanied by pus and loss of skin depth.

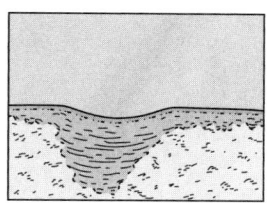

A(n) _____ is a slightly raised mark on the skin formed after an injury or lesion of the skin has healed.

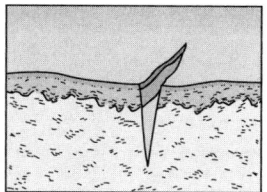

A(n) _____ is a narrow opening or furrow in the skin.

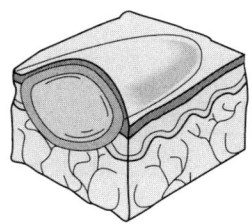

A(n) _____ is a small, bump beneath the surface of the skin that can be caused by infections, scar tissue, and fatty deposits.

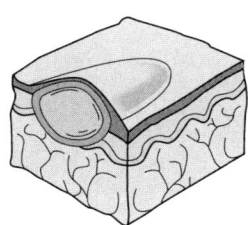

A(n) _____ is a closed, abnormally developed sac containing fluid, infection, or other matter above or below the skin.

TOPIC 3: SEBACEOUS GLAND DISORDERS

1. Match the following terms with the sebaceous gland disorders described below.

comedone	milia	acne	asteatosis	sebaceous hyperplasia
steatoma/wen	seborrheic dermatitis	furuncle/boil	seborrhea	

a) _____: chronic inflammatory skin disorder of the sebaceous glands characterized by comedones and blemishes

b) _____: dry, scaly skin due to sebum deficiency

c) _____: skin condition caused by an inflammation of the sebaceous glands

d) _____: sebaceous abscess filled with pus

e) _____: whitish, pearl-like masses of sebum and dead cells under the skin with no visible opening

f) _____: overgrowth of the sebaceous glands

g) _____: sebaceous cyst or subcutaneous tumor filled with sebum

h) _____: non-inflamed buildup of cells

i) _____: severe oiliness of the skin

2. What is the medical term for each of the following skin conditions?

   a) blackheads: _____

   b) dry, scaly skin: _____

   c) whiteheads: _____

   d) oily skin: _____

3. Describe sebaceous hyperplasia. _____
   _____

4. Is acne considered to be an acute or a chronic disease? _____

5. A steatoma is a subcutaneous tumor of the sebaceous glands.

   a) Where does a steatoma usually occur? _____

   b) What are the characteristics of steatoma? _____

6. What is generally thought to be the cause of asteatosis? _____
   _____

7. A furuncle or _____ is caused by _____ in glands or hair follicles.

8. Give the primary indication of a cyst. _____
   _____

Rapid Review Test

Date: _____

Rating: _____

Word Review

acne	cyst	raised
acute	furuncle	carbuncle
asteatosis debris	hair follicle	secretion
blackheads	lesion	sebaceous
clogged	milia	steatoma
chronic	pus	wen
comedones	pustule	whitehead

Match the following terms with their descriptions below.

acne	milia	sebaceous hyperplasia
alkalies	rosacea	seborrhea
asteatosis	sebaceous	subcutaneous
comedone		

1. A blackhead is an open _____.

2. Severe oiliness of the skin is referred to as _____.

3. Asteatosis is a dry skin condition often caused by products containing _____.

4. A furuncle is a _____ abscess filled with pus.

5. _____ is an overgrowth of the sebaceous gland that can be removed only by surgery.

6. Whiteheads are also known as _____.

7. A chronic inflammatory disorder usually affecting the nose and cheeks is called _____.

8. A steatoma is also called a _____ cyst.

9. _____ is a chronic inflammatory disorder of the sebaceous glands.

10. Scaly, dry skin due to aging or body disorder is known as _____.

TOPIC 4: DISORDERS OF THE SUDORIFEROUS (SWEAT) GLANDS

1. Describe the following sudoriferous disorders:

    a) miliaria rubra: _____

    b) bromhidrosis: _____

    c) hyperhidrosis: _____

    d) anhidrosis: _____

Rapid Review Test

Date:_____

Rating: _____

Word Review

Match the following terms with their descriptions below.

| excessive | fever |
| yeast | red vesicles |

1. Miliaria rubra results in the eruption of _____.

2. Bromhidrosis is caused by bacteria and _____.

3. Hyperhydrosis is characterized by _____ sweating.

4. Anhidrosis is often the result of skin disease or _____.

TOPIC 5: INFLAMMATIONS OF THE SKIN

1. Match the following terms with the inflammation descriptions below.

psoriasis	urticaria	pruitis	erythema	eczema	dermatitis	atopic dermatitis
rosacea	folliculitis	telangiectasia	edema	contact dermatitis	perioral dermatitis	

a) _____: vascular lesion

b) _____: characterized by red patches covered with white-silver scales

c) _____: ingrown hairs

d) _____: inflammation of the skin characterized by redness, dilation of blood vessels, and in severe cases, the formation of papules and pustules

e) _____: also known as hives

f) _____: medical term for itching

g) _____: inflammatory condition caused by contact with a substance or chemical

h) _____: acne-like condition around the mouth

i) _____: swelling from a fluid imbalance in the cells

j) _____: rash

k) _____: redness due to inflammation

l) _____: inflammatory, painful, itching diseases, acute or chronic in nature

m) _____: inflammatory condition of the skin

2. List three types of skin lesions that are usually found in dermatitis.

   a) _____

   b) _____

   c) _____

3. An _____ is an immune system response caused by repeated exposure to an allergen.

4. Name the likely places for allergic contact dermatitis to occur in clients and technicians.

   a) _____

   b) _____

   c) _____

5. _____ affects everyone who comes in contact with an irritant.

6. What are the two basic signs of eczema?

   a) _____

   b) _____

7. What are the usual signs of psoriasis? _____

8. Razor bumps are often referred to as _____.

Rapid Review Test

Date: _____

Rating: _____

Word Review

Match the following terms with their descriptions below.

venenata	erythema	contact dermatitis
edema	psoriasis	dermatitis
pruitis	mouth	ingrown hairs
atopic dermatitis	dilation	hives

1. _____ is a skin condition characterized by silvery scales.

2. An allergic reaction from contact with a substance or chemical is called _____.

3. Swelling is called _____.
4. Redness caused by inflammation is called _____.
5. _____ is the medical term for various forms of lesions affecting the skin.
6. Occupational disorders such as dermatitis _____ can be caused by contact with chemicals.
7. _____ is the medical term for itching.
8. Perioral dermatitis is characterized by an acne-like condition around the _____.
9. Folliculitis is the medical term for _____.
10. Redness, itching, and dehydration of the dermatitis makes _____ worse.
11. Rosacea is characterized by redness and by _____ of the vessels.
12. Urticaria is the medical term for _____.

TOPIC 6: PIGMENTATION DISORDERS

1. Abnormal conditions involving skin pigmentation may be due to _____ or _____ causes.
2. Hyperpigmentation disorders include:
    a) _____: increased pigmentation; liver spots
    b) _____: overproduction of pigment due to sun exposure, acne, medications and post-inflammatory reactions
    c) _____: freckle(s)
    d) _____: term for hyperpigmentation; can be triggered by hormonal changes
    e) _____: birthmark or mole
    f) _____: brown or wine-colored discoloration
    g) _____: change in pigmentation due to melanin production as a defense against UV rays
3. _____ denotes a lack of pigment.

Rapid Review Test

Date: _____

Rating: _____

Word Review

Match the following terms with their descriptions below.

| albinism | stain | leukoderma | freckle |
| vitiligo | hypopigmentation | hyperpigmentation | vitiligo |

1. _____ are white spots caused by a lack of pigment cells.
2. _____ is abnormal light patches on the skin caused by congenital disease.
3. _____ is the absence of melanin pigment in the body.
4. _____ a lack of pigment.
5. _____ occur after certain diseases.
6. Melasma is the medical term for _____.
7. Lentigo is one _____.
8. _____ is worsened by sunlight.

True or False

1. _____ Hyperpigmentation denotes a lack of pigmentation.

2. _____ Chloasma is the medical term for freckles.

3. _____ A birthmark or mole is called a nevus.

4. _____ A port wine stain is a vascular lesion.

5. _____ The absence of melanin pigment in the body is called albinism.

6. _____ Vitiligo is characterized by white spots on the skin.

7. _____ Leukoderma is characterized by dark, abnormal patches on the skin.

TOPIC 7: HYPERTROPHIES

1. Match the following terms with their definitions below.

actinic keratoses	keratosis pilaris	skin tag
keratoma	mole	verruca

   a) _____: acquired thickened patch of epidermis
   b) _____: brownish spot that can be flat or raised
   c) _____: commonly called a wart
   d) _____: small, flaplike extension of the skin
   e) _____: rough, pink or flesh-toned precancerous lesions from sun damage
   f) _____: bumpiness in the cheeks and upper arms

2. Calluses are _____.
3. A thickening of the skin caused by a mass of keratinized cells is called a _____.
4. Keratosis pilaris is caused by _____.
5. A verruca or _____ is caused by a virus and is _____ or infectious.
6. Common areas for skin tags are _____.

Rapid Review Test

Date: _____

Rating: _____

True or False

1. _____ Many hypertrophies are harmless.

2. _____ Hyperkeratosis is a thinning of the skin.

3. _____ Hairs in moles need to be removed.

4. _____ A wart is a hypertrophy of the papillae and epidermis caused by a bacteria.

5. _____ Exfoliation can help alleviate the roughness associated with keratosis pilaris.

TOPIC 8: SKIN CANCER

1. _____ means not harmful; _____ means cancerous.
2. Each form of cancer is named for the type of _____ that are affected.
3. Skin cancer tumors form when _____.
4. _____ is rising faster than any other cancer.
5. More than _____ percent of all skin cancers are caused by sun exposure.
6. Do clouds block UV rays? _____
7. _____ is the most common, and the least severe, type of skin cancer.
8. _____ is characterized by red or pink scaly papules or nodules; it can spread to other areas of the body.
9. _____ is characterized by black or dark patches that are usually uneven in texture, jagged, or raised. It can be tan or white.
10. _____ is the most serious type of skin cancer.
11. The ABCDE method of recognizing potential skin cancers includes:
    a) A: _____
    b) B: _____
    c) C: _____
    d) D: _____
    e) E: _____

Rapid Review Test

Date: _____

Rating: _____

True or False

1. _____ Squamous cell carcinoma is less serious than basal cell carcinoma.

2. _____ Malignant melanoma is a very serious disease, but it is rarely fatal.

3. _____ Basal cell carcinoma does not spread easily.

4. _____ The American Cancer Society recommends using the ABCDE Cancer Checklist to make skin cancer easier to recognize.

5. _____ Using a tanning bed is safer than tanning outdoors because it offers controlled exposure to UV rays.

TOPIC 9: CONTAGIOUS DISEASES

1. The term *contagious disease* is used interchangeably with the terms _____.

2. Match the following terms with their descriptions below.

| tinea corporis | tinea versicolor | verruca | herpes zoster |
| tinea | herpes simplex virus | bacterial conjunctivitis | impetigo |

   a) _____: fever blisters or cold sores caused by a recurring viral infection
   b) _____: fungal infection inhibiting melanin production
   c) _____: bacterial infection of the skin; often occurs in children
   d) _____: shingles
   e) _____: fungal infections
   f) _____: highly contagious ringworm
   g) _____: pink eye
   h) _____: warts

3. _____ is characterized by fever blisters or cold sores.
4. The medical name for genital herpes is _____.
5. _____ is a highly contagious disease characterized by clusters of small blisters or crusty lesions filled with bacteria.
6. Tinea versicolor is also called _____.
7. Verrucas are caused by _____; they are characterized by _____ of the papillae and epidermis.
8. _____ is commonly called pinkeye.
9. Herpes zoster is a painful skin condition caused by the _____ virus.
10. The common name for tinea pedis is _____.

Rapid Review Test

Date: _____

Rating: _____

True or False

1. _____ You should wear gloves when performing a facial on someone with a contagious disease.

2. _____ Bacterial conjunctivitis can be spread through contaminated makeup.

3. _____ Impetigo is a bacterial infection characterized by small blisters or crusty lesions filled with bacteria.

4. _____ Tinea corporis, or ringworm, is caused by wormlike parasites that form a ringed red pattern with elevated edges.

5. _____ Actinic keratoses are also known as skin tags.

6. _____ Verrucas, or warts, are contagious.

7. _____ Herpes zoster, or shingles, is caused by the chickenpox virus.

8. _____ *Tinea* is the medical term for a fungal infection.

TOPIC 10: ACNE

1. What is acne? _____
2. Causes of acne include:
    a) _____
    b) _____
    c) _____
    d) _____
3. _____ is a hereditary factor in which dead skin cells do not shed from the follicles as they do on normal skin.
4. Name the two types of follicles in the skin. _____
5. _____ are mainly solidified impactions of oil without the cell matter.
6. Bacteria in follicles are _____, which means _____.
7. When follicles are blocked with sebum and dead skin buildup, oxygen cannot reach the bottom of the follicle, causing a _____.
8. Cysts are nodules made up of _____.
9. Male hormones, known as _____, stimulate _____ glands.
10. Is adult acne more common in males or females? _____
11. Hormonal fluctuations from _____ can all lead to acne.
12. _____ in cosmetics can clog pores or irritate follicles.
13. _____ breakouts are caused by pressure or friction.
14. Acne grades are determined by _____ present.
15. The four acne grades are:
    a) Grade 1: _____
    b) Grade II: _____

67

c) Grade III: _____
   d) Grade IV: _____
16. Adapalene®, Retin-A®, Tazorac®, and Azelex® are _____ acne treatments that are prescribed by a physician.
17. Accutane® is an _____ medication similar to retinoic acid that is prescribed by physicians for severe acne.

Rapid Review Test
Date: _____

Rating: _____

Word Review

Match the following terms with their descriptions below.

acne triggers	inflammation	pilosebaceous	androgens
papules	comedogenic	cystic acne	sebaceous filaments

1. _____: hormonal changes, stress, products, foods, climate, sun
2. _____: stimulate sebaceous glands
3. _____: similar to open comedones
4. _____: can be caused by sebum
5. _____: red, inflamed lesions
6. _____: must be treated by a physician
7. _____: causes cell buildup
8. _____: entire follicle

Date: _____

Rating: _____

Text pages: 234–251

CHAPTER 11
Skin analysis

TOPIC 1: SKIN TYPES

1. _____ and _____ generally determine skin type.

2. A client's _____ is primarily based on how much oil is produced in the follicles and on the amount of _____ found between the cells.

3. Skin that is lacking oil is called _____.

4. Generally, what size are the follicles of dry skin? _____

5. What is the purpose of occlusive products? _____

6. Describe the difference between "dry skin" and "dehydrated skin." _____

7. Describe the characteristics of the pores of normal skin. _____

8. What is the purpose of a skin care regimen for normal skin? _____

9. Combination skin can be both _____ or _____ at the same time.

10. List the three areas included in the T-zone.

    a) _____

    b) _____

    c) _____

11. Are water-based or oil-based products best suited for combination skin? _____

12. List two characteristics of oily skin.

    a) _____

    b) _____

13. What is the goal when treating this type of skin? _____

14. What can make oily skin worse? _____

    Why? _____

15. Sensitive skin is both a _____ and a _____.

16. List the three most common characteristics of sensitive skin:

    a) _____

    b) _____

    c) _____

17. Fragile or thin skin can be the result of _____ or _____.
18. Provide descriptions for the following Fitzpatrick skin types.
    a) Type I: _____
    b) Type II: _____
    c) Type III: _____
    d) Type IV: _____
    e) Type V: _____
    f) Type VI: _____
19. Which Fitzpatrick skin type always burns, never tans? _____
20. Which Fitzpatrick skin type sometimes burns, gradually tans? _____
21. Which Fitzpatrick skin types always tan? _____
22. Black skin needs more exfoliation and deep pore cleansing due to its susceptibility to _____.
23. Darker skin types are prone to develop post-inflammatory _____.
24. What ethnic skin type is considered to be one of the most sensitive? _____

Rapid Review Test

Date: _____

Rating: _____

1. Insert the correct term in the space provided.

alipidic	melanin	dehydrated
color	hyperpigmentation	sensitive

    a) Skin lacking oil is called _____.
    b) Skin that is _____ can be found in all skin types.
    c) Low tolerance to products and stimulation are characteristics of _____ skin.
    d) _____ gives the skin its _____ and protection from the sun.
    e) Darker skin is prone to _____.
2. Ethnic skin types typically have thicker _____ and need more _____.
3. Insert the correct term in the space provided.

combination	dry	normal
combination	mature/aging	oily
couperose	sensitive skin	ethnic

    a) _____: skin in good condition with a sufficient supply of sebum and moisture
    b) _____: skin having both dry and oily areas
    c) _____: skin lacking oil
    d) _____: skin generally loose, wrinkled, or lined
    e) _____: skin identified by distended capillaries
    f) _____: skin with an overabundance of sebum
    g) _____: needs to be balanced and requires more care than normal skin
    h) _____: does not show aging as quickly as Caucasian skin
    i) _____: couperose skin conditions are noticeable

TOPIC 3: SKIN TYPES VERSUS SKIN CONDITIONS

Name at least eight of the most common skin conditions that an esthetician focuses on.

1. _____
2. _____
3. _____
4. _____
5. _____
6. _____
7. _____
8. _____
9. _____
10. _____
11. _____
12. _____
13. _____

Match the following terms with their descriptions below.

cysts	enlarged pores	irritation	hyperkeratinization	papules
solar comedones	adult acne	dehydration	actinic keratosis	pustules
sun damage	keratosis/keratoses	sensitivities	poor elasticity	milia
seborrhea	telangiectasias	erythema	couperose skin	wrinkles/aging
comedones	asphyxiated	hypopigmentation	hyperpigmentation	rosacea

1. _____: redness, distended capillaries from weakening of the capillary walls
2. _____: open: blackheads; closed: whiteheads; not open to the air/oxygen
3. _____: lack of water
4. _____: acne breakouts from hormonal changes or other factors
5. _____: expansion due to elasticity loss or trauma
6. _____: lack of oxygen
7. _____: excessive buildup of dead skin cells/keratinized cells
8. _____: distended capillaries from weakening of the capillary walls
9. _____: rough area that appears from sun exposure; may have a layered scale or scab that sometimes falls off.
10. _____: discoloration from melanin production due to sun, other factors, or irritation
11. _____: infected papule with fluid inside
12. _____: large blackheads around the eyes from sun exposure
13. _____: lines and damage from internal or external causes
14. _____: UV damage to the epidermis and dermis
15. _____: fluid, infection, or other matter under the skin
16. _____: hardened whiteheads with no visible opening
17. _____: redness caused by inflammation
18. _____: white, colorless areas from lack of melanin production
19. _____: raised lesions/blemishes

20. _____: vascular disorder; chronic redness; papules and pustules may be present
21. _____: buildup of cells; a rough texture
22. _____: usually redness or inflammation from a variety of causes
23. _____: reactions from internal or external causes
24. _____: severe oiliness of the skin
25. _____: sagging; loose skin from damage, sun, and aging

Rapid Review Test

Date: _____

Rating: _____

True or False

1. _____ Skin conditions are determined only by our genetic makeup.

2. _____ Asphyxiated skin is common among smokers.

3. _____ Hormonal imbalances can negatively affect the capillaries.

4. _____ Dry skin and dehydrated skin mean the same thing.

5. _____ Sensitive skin is both a skin type and a skin condition.

6. _____ Skin conditions are of primary importance to estheticians.

7. _____ Gentler exfoliation products such as enzymes are recommended for Asian skin.

8. _____ Native American, Indian, and Hispanic skin require different care and precautions than other ethnic skin types.

9. _____ Abnormal hypertrophic scarring (keloids) are less problematic for black skin.

TOPIC 4: FACTORS THAT AFFECT THE SKIN

1. _____, _____, and _____ all play a part in our health, which in turn is reflected in our skin's appearance.
2. There are many internal and external factors that cause skin conditions. Place an "I" for intrinsic or "E" for extrinsic in the space provided for each of the following causes.
   ___ a) dehydration
   ___ b) genetics/ethnicity-influenced conditions
   ___ c) environmental exposure/pollutants/air quality

___ d) oral medications, drugs

___ e) environment/humidity

___ f) hormones/menopause

___ g) allergies/reactions to environmental factors or products

___ h) stress, lifestyle, negative attitude

___ i) improper nutrition, alcohol, caffeine

___ j) misuse of products or treatments

___ k) vitamin deficiency

___ l) sun damage

___ m) lack of exercise

___ n) smoking

___ o) poor maintenance/home care

___ p) medical conditions

___ q) lack of rest/sleep

___ r) free radicals

3. Hormonal imbalances can lead to _____ _____ that affect the capillaries.
4. _____ is the main external cause of aging.
5. Incorrect _____ analysis and _____ recommendations can lead to skin problems.
6. Sunlight is _____.
7. UVB rays have shorter _____ and are _____ than UVA rays.
8. UVC rays are more _____, but they are mainly absorbed by the _____.
9. UVA rays have _____ wavelengths that penetrate _____ than UVB rays.
10. MED is the term used to describe the _____.
11. MED calculates how long it takes to become _____ or develop _____ from sun exposure.
12. Erythema is the result of _____ in the dermis.

Rapid Review Test

Date: _____

Rating: _____

True or False

1. _____ Smoking, lack of rest or exercise, and menopause are all intrinsic factors in the health and appearance of the skin.

2. _____ Extrinsic factors include free radicals, dehydration, medications and lack of exercise.

3. _____ UVB rays are known as the burning rays.

TOPIC 5: HEALTHY HABITS FOR THE SKIN

1. Preventive measures are the best approach to maintaining vital skin. List at least six preventive measures that promote healthier skin.

   a) _____
   b) _____
   c) _____
   d) _____
   e) _____
   f) _____
   g) _____
   h) _____
   i) _____

Activity

List 10 skin care habits that you could change to improve the health of your skin. Be specific on how you are going to do this. Share your list with the class.

TOPIC 6: CONTRAINDICATIONS

1. _____ are circumstances that could cause harmful or negative _____ to those who have specific medical or skin conditions.
2. Contagious diseases, skin disorders, medical conditions, medications, and skin irritation can all ____ _____ a service.
3. _____ you may not ask clients about contagious diseases, but they may list them on the _____.
4. Which types of products/medications are contraindications for waxing, exfoliation/peeling, or stimulating treatments? _____
5. _____ are contraindications for electrical and light treatments.
6. Clients who have pacemakers, heart irregularities, or metal bone pins or plates should never receive _____.
7. Clients who are taking blood thinners should not receive _____.
8. Clients with multiple allergies should always use _____ products designed for _____ skin.
9. Pregnant clients should not receive electrical treatments, or any _____, without the written consent of a physician.
10. Clients suffering from _____, such as lupus, should never receive _____ or _____ treatments.
11. Diabetics _____ very slowly and may not readily feel _____. If you have any questions, you should get approval from the _____ before treatment.

Rapid Review Test

Date: _____

Rating: _____

Word Review

Match the following terms to their descriptions below.

| epilepsy | multiple allergies | metal plates | pacemaker | prednisone |
| pregnancy | diabetics | Renova® | lupus | |

1. _____: avoid all electrical treatments
2. _____; avoid all electrical treatments
3. _____: avoid all electrical treatments
4. _____: use fragrance-free products designed for sensitive skin
5. _____: avoid waxing, any exfoliation or peeling treatment, or stimulating treatment
6. _____: may not feel pain, particularly in the feet
7. _____: avoid all electrical treatments and light treatments
8. _____: avoid electrical treatments; harsh treatments of any kind
9. _____: avoid waxing, any exfoliation or peeling treatment, or stimulating treatment

TOPIC 7: CONSULTATIONS, CLIENT CHARTS, AND HEALTH SCREENING

1. The most important reasons to conduct a thorough consultation is to know about any _____ _____ the clients may have.
2. Contraindications include any _____.
3. Clients should fill out these forms: _____.
4. A _____ releases you from liability before you perform services.
5. A _____ is where you record all of your notes from the skin analysis, what you used in the treatment, and your home-care recommendations.
6. Important questions to ask during the consultation include:
    a) _____
    b) _____
    c) _____
    d) _____
    e) _____
    f) _____
    g) _____
7. Client information is personal and _____.
8. Knowing how to _____ skin is the first step in providing skin care.
9. A _____ of treatments may be necessary to effectively help the client's conditions.
10. Knowing about skin types, conditions, and the factors affecting the skin's health enables you to give an accurate _____.
11. Using a _____ is recommended when analyzing the skin.
12. Note the following details in a skin analysis: _____.
13. Besides a visual analysis, use your _____ to touch the skin.

14. Skin analysis checklist:

    a) _____: Check the pore size and oil distribution.

    b) _____: Note the comedones, capillaries, pigmentation, sun damage, and other conditions.

    c) _____: Is the skin dry, clear, oily, red, irritated? What else do you notice?

    d) _____: Is the texture rough, smooth, dehydrated, firm? Record your observations on the client's chart.

15. You cannot do an accurate analysis if your client is wearing _____.

16. In your own words, list the steps of a skin care analysis:

    a) _____

    b) _____

    c) _____

    d) _____

    e) _____

    f) _____

    g) _____

17. What are the four components of skin analysis? _____

Activity

Have students pair up and conduct consultations on each other. Ask a third student to grade their consultations based on covering all the steps listed above.

Word Review

abnormalities	cysts	magnifying lamp
allergy	diagnose	medication
analyze	examine	microcirculation
asphyxiated	eyepads	occlusive
consultation	flakiness	Wood's lamp
comedone	follicle	texture
condition	hydrated	T-zone
contraindication	keratosis	lipids

Date: _____

Rating: _____

Text pages: 252–294

CHAPTER 12
Skin Care Products: Chemistry, Ingredients, and Selection

TOPIC 1: COSMETIC CHEMISTRY AND INGREDIENTS

1. The Food and Drug Administration (FDA) views cosmetics according to the _____, which distinguishes between _____.

2. _____ are defined by the FDA as "articles that are intended to be rubbed, poured, sprinkled or otherwise applied to the human body or any part thereof for cleansing, beautifying, promoting attractiveness or alternating the appearance."

3. _____ allow products to spread, give them body and texture, and give them a specific form such as a lotion, cream, or gel.

4. _____ cause the actual changes in the appearance of skin.

5. _____ are a proposed third category (FDA); they are intended to improve the skin's health and appearance.

6. Ingredients can be derived from _____.

7. _____ describes ingredients that may be less likely to cause allergic reactions.

8. _____ describes ingredients that will not clog pores or cause comedones.

9. What is the most frequently used cosmetic ingredient? _____

10. As a performance ingredient, water _____.

11. Products that do not contain any water are called _____.

12. Fatty materials used to lubricate and moisture the face are called _____.

13. Emollients in loose powder help the powder to _____.

14. As performance drugs, _____ lubricate the skin's surface and set up a guard for the barrier functions.

15. Mineral oil and petrolatum come from the _____.

16. Plant oils contain _____, which are beneficial for skin that does not produce enough sebum.

17. _____ are lubricant ingredients derived from plant oils or animal fats.

18. When fatty acids have been exposed to hydrogen, they become _____.

19. _____ are produced from fatty acids and fatty alcohols.

20. What group of oils is chemically combined with silicon and oxygen? _____

21. Dimethicone, cyclomethicone, and phenyl trimethicone are examples of _____.

22. Comedogenicity is the tendency of any topical substance to cause or to worsen a _____.

23. Which category of ingredients reduces the surface tension between the skin and the product? _____

24. The main type of surfactant used in cleansing agents is _____.

25. Without _____, oil and water would separate into layers.
26. _____ gives products a gel-like consistency.
27. _____ is the therapeutic use of plant aromas and essential oils for beauty and health treatment purposes.
28. What prevents bacteria and other microorganisms from living in a product? _____
29. What type of ingredient is added to products to improve the efficiency of a preservative? _____
30. The _____ regulates color agent ingredients.
31. Certified colors are listed on ingredient labels as _____.
32. What are lakes? _____
33. Which colors do not require certification? _____
34. Match the following terms with their descriptions below.

hydrators	botanicals/phytotherapy	solvents
pH adjusters		

   a) _____: alkaline and acid bases that adjust the pH of products
   b) _____: ingredients derived from plants that benefit the skin
   c) _____: also known as humectants
   d) _____: substances such as water that are used to dissolve other ingredients

35. Exfoliation can be achieved through _____ actions.
36. _____ physically scrape dead cells from the skin's surface.
37. Alpha hydroxy acids are used to _____ exfoliate the skin.
38. Papain, bromelain, and pancreatin are all _____ that gently exfoliate the skin.
39. _____ are ingredients used in the bleaching or lightening of the skin.
40. _____ converts tyrosine into melanin.
41. Which chemical systems deliver ingredients to specific tissues of the epidermis? _____
42. Water and emollients are _____ that carry other ingredients into the skin.
43. What are liposomes? What is their purpose? _____
44. Which delivery system releases substances onto the skin's surface at a microscopically controlled rate? _____
45. What is the proper name for microsponges? _____
46. Vitamins C and E, green tea, and DMAE are _____.
47. Polyglucans are _____, therefore helping to preserve and protect collagen and elastin.
48. Beta-glucans help reduce the appearance of fine lines and wrinkles by _____.
49. _____ is derived from yeast cells and functions as an anti-inflammatory and moisturizing ingredient.
50. Glycoproteins are derived from _____.
51. _____ are chains of amino acids used in skin care products to produce changes in the appearance of the skin.

52. _____ is a natural form of vitamin A.

53. Retinoic acid is a form of vitamin A that is of the keratolytic group. What does this mean? _____

54. Vitamins C and E, alphalipoic acid, idebenone, and coenzyme Q-10 are all _____.

55. There are two types of sunscreen ingredients: _____.

56. Chemical sunscreens chemically _____ ultraviolet rays.

57. Physical sunscreens _____ ultraviolet rays.

58. The FDA regulates cosmetics in terms of _____, _____, and _____.

59. Cosmetic ingredients are listed in _____ order of predominance, starting with the ingredient that has the _____ concentration.

60. What should you do after applying a product if the skin becomes excessively red or the client complains of burning? _____

61. Before a treatment, it is a good idea to _____ any client who has reactive skin.

62. Aromatherapy is a(n) _____ healing practice.

63. Aromatherapy treats the _____.

64. _____ is the use of plant extracts for therapeutic benefits.

65. _____ are the main focus of the skin care industry.

66. _____ neutralize the damaging effects of free radicals.

67. Vitamin C strengthens the _____ and is essential for producing _____.

68. Dimethylaminoethanol is commonly called _____.

69. Vitamins A and E protect the _____.

Rapid Review Test

Date: _____

Rating: _____

1. Match the following natural ingredients with their benefits listed below.

| aromatherapy oils | pomegranate | lemongrass | avocado | cucumber | witch hazel |
| honey | comfrey root | phytotherapy | rose | zinc oxide | seaweed |

　　a) _____: rich in vitamins and oil; beneficial for dry and sensitive skin

　　b) _____: use of plant extracts for therapeutic benefits

　　c) _____: physical sunscreen ingredient; reflects UVA rays

　　d) _____: treat the mind, body, and spirit

　　e) _____: calming

　　f) _____: cleansing

　　g) _____: hydrating, toning

　　h) _____: moisturizing

　　i) _____: powerful antioxidant; treats sun damage

　　j) _____: astringent and antiseptic

　　k) _____: humectant and moisturizing properties; firming

　　l) _____: soothing and healing; commonly used as a mask or for eye pads

2. Match the following ingredients with their benefits listed below.

parabens	squalene	sphingolipids	ceramides	hyaluronic acid	mucopolysaccharides
salicylic acid	alum	retinoic acid	squalane	potassium hydroxide	

a) _____: one of the most commonly used groups of preservatives

b) _____: vitamin A derivative

c) _____: has excellent water-binding properties

d) _____: carbohydrate–lipid complexes, good water binders

e) _____: beta hydroxy acid with exfoliating and antiseptic properties

f) _____: lipid materials found in skin's intercellular cement

g) _____: good for oily skin

h) _____: derived from olives

i) _____: obtained from shark liver oil

k) _____: lipids

l) _____: strong alkali used in soaps and creams

True or False

1. _____ According to the FDA, cosmeceuticals are products intended to affect the structures and/or functions of the body.

2. _____ Lips balms and oil serums are anhydrous.

3. _____ Emollients are fatty materials used to lubricate and moisturize the skin. They should never be used in loose powder cosmetics.

4. _____ Lubricants coat the skin and increase friction.

5. _____ Plant oils contain fatty acids.

6. _____ Comedogenic ingredients clog the follicles and should always be avoided when making your product selections.

7. _____ Emulsifiers make it possible for oil particles to remain evenly distributed throughout the water.

8. _____ A chelating agent prevents a buildup of oils on the skin.

9. _____ PH adjustors are acids or alkalis used to adjust the pH of products.

10. _____ Solvents dissolve other substances.

11. _____ Lipids can reduce sensitivity by making the skin more resistant to irritants and dehydration.

12. _____ Tyrozinase is a lipid that converts tyrosine, an amino acid, into melanin.

13. _____ The FDA requires cosmetics to be proven safe and effective before their manufacture and sale.

14. Separate the following terms into the appropriate categories listed below:

| coenzyme Q-10 | liposomes | vitamin C | polymers | TRF | green tea |
| glycoproteins | vitamin E | Beta-glucans | glycyrrhizinate | idebenone | polyglucans |

a) Improves cell metabolism and oxygenation:

_____
_____
_____
_____

b) Delivery systems:

_____
_____

c) Antioxidants:

_____
_____
_____
_____
_____
_____
_____

TOPIC 2: PRODUCT SELECTION

1. Name the main categories in skin care products.

    a) _____
    b) _____
    c) _____
    d) _____
    e) _____
    f) _____
    g) _____

2. Cleansers should leave the skin _____ balanced.

3. Cleansers _____ makeup and dirt to keep _____ clean and _____ for other products.

4. What are the three basic forms of cleansers?

   a) _____

   b) _____

   c) _____

5. Describe the purpose of a cleansing gel: _____.

6. What is the most important caution to consider when recommending a cleansing gel? _____

7. Describe a cleansing lotion. _____
   _____

8. Milky cleansing lotions are used by which skin type? _____

9. Describe the purposes of a cleansing cream. _____
   _____

10. Are makeup removers generally oil-based or water-based? _____

11. _____ usually have a higher alcohol content and are designed for use on normal and combination skin.

12. _____ have the highest alcohol content and are used for oily and acne-prone skin.

13. _____ often have the lowest alcohol content and are beneficial for dry, mature, and sensitive skin.

14. List at least six general benefits of exfoliating the skin:

    a) _____

    b) _____

    c) _____

    d) _____

    e) _____

    f) _____

    g) _____

    h) _____

15. List the skin conditions that benefit from exfoliation:

    a) _____

    b) _____

    c) _____

16. What does exfoliation refer to? _____

17. _____ is a method of physically rubbing dead cells off the skin.

18. _____ dissolves the intercellular glue by using chemical agents such as AHAs.

19. How do enzymes remove dead skin cells? _____

20. Contraindications for harsh mechanical peel techniques, scrubs, and brushing machines include:

    a) _____

    b) _____

    c) _____

    d) _____

    e) _____

    f) _____

21. Gommage is a cream type of _____ peel that is removed by _____.

22. Masks and packs offer many benefits. List seven advantages of using these products.

   a) _____
   b) _____
   c) _____
   d) _____
   e) _____
   f) _____
   g) _____

23. There are two mask categories: _____

24. _____ masks harden or dry and provide a complete barrier on top of the skin; _____ _____ masks stay moist and are more hydrating.

25. Nonsetting masks are also referred to as _____ or _____. They are formulated to _____

26. Clay masks draw _____ to the surface of the skin as they dry and _____.

27. Alginate masks are often _____ based, and dry to form a _____ texture.

28. Paraffin wax masks are used to _____ and _____.

29. Paraffin wax masks are not recommended for use on _____.

30. What is another name for thermal masks? _____

31. What causes the increased temperature in thermal masks? _____

32. When do you apply serums and ampoules? _____

33. Why do serums penetrate deeper into the skin? _____

34. What are ampoules? _____

35. List the benefits of eye creams:

   a) _____
   b) _____
   c) _____
   d) _____

36. Eye creams are usually _____ to protect thin, delicate tissue.

37. _____ include moisturizing balms and products with collagen derivatives to _____ up the lips.

38. Benefits of hydrators and moisturizers include:

   a) _____
   b) _____
   c) _____
   d) _____

39. Lotions, hydrators, and creams are known as _____.

40. Hydrators are formulated with _____ to attract water to the skin.

83

41. Oil-based moisturizers contain _____. They are heavier and occlusive to _____ and _____ under the cream.

42. Why does oily skin need hydration? _____

43. Treatment creams and massage lotions are different forms of _____.

44. Treatment creams are also referred to as _____.

45. Treatment creams are often _____ in consistency than moisturizers and contain more _____ and _____ ingredients.

46. What are massage creams designed to do? _____

47. What six negative results can occur when the skin is not protected from ultraviolet rays?
    a) _____
    b) _____
    c) _____
    d) _____
    e) _____
    f) _____

48. A _____ sunscreen protects against UVA and UVB rays.

49. Sunscreens _____ UV rays.

50. SPF refers to the _____ in sunscreens.

51. Increasing the _____ in sunscreens increases the protection.

52. What is the active ingredient in self-tanning lotions? _____

Rapid Review Test

Date: _____

Rating: _____

Word Review

Match the following terms with their descriptions below.

cleansers	keratolytic	cleansing gel	custom-designed
fresheners	oxybenzone	titanium dioxide	serums
astringents	mechanical	paraffin	UVB rays
enzyme	modelage	chemical	UVA rays

1. _____ exfoliants dissolve the intercellular glue that holds the dead skin cells together.
2. _____ are responsible for skin aging.
3. _____ exfoliants digest the dead cells on the surface.
4. _____ help oily and acneic conditions and remove excess oil on the skin.
5. _____ masks are also called thermal masks.
6. _____ masks are not recommended for sensitive, oily, or acneic skin.
7. _____ are recommended for dry, mature, and sensitive skin.
8. _____ come in three basic forms: gels, lotions, and creams.
9. _____ are the primary cause of skin cancer.

10. _____ is a detergent type of foaming cleanser.
11. _____ enzymes help speed up the breakdown of keratin.
12. _____ are concentrated ingredients that target specific skin conditions.
13. _____ masks are homemade from ingredients such as honey and yogurt.
14. _____ in sunscreens helps shield the skin from UVA rays.
15. _____ exfoliation includes microdermabrasion and scrubs.
16. _____ is a sunscreen ingredient that protects against UVB rays.

Activity

Using the charts in your textbook, develop a home regimen plan for oily, normal, dry, mature, sensitive, acneic, and combination skin types. Get creative! (These products do not have to exist; you may create them.) Use herbs, oils, extracts, and so on as additives (example: toner with spearmint extract).

TOPIC 3: HOME-CARE PRODUCTS

1. It is a good idea to give a _____ to those clients who may not remember what you told them.
2. Retail sales are not just about money; you are helping clients to _____.
3. Give _____ instructions as to how and when to use the product.
4. While professional products may cost more, they are usually more _____ because of a _____ of performance ingredients.

TOPIC 4: CHOOSING A PRODUCT LINE

1. Deciding on which product lines to use and retail can be one of the biggest _____ an esthetician has to make.
2. List at least six selling points to consider when choosing a product line:
    a) _____
    b) _____
    c) _____
    d) _____
    e) _____
    f) _____
    g) _____
    h) _____
3. Generally the markup for a retail product is _____ percent.

Activity

Divide your class into two or three teams, depending on the number of students. Have the teams identify a popular skin care brand that they like and recommend. Each team should then investigate the range of products they will need for retail purposes; their total cost (do not forget shipping, taxes, and minimum order requirements); and their retail prices. Have them estimate (1) how long it will take to sell out of their retail products, and (2) the profit they would gain from the sales.

Date: _____

Rating: _____

Text pages: 295–311

CHAPTER 13

The Treatment Room

TOPIC 1: ESTHETICIAN'S PRESENTATION

1. Making a good first _____ is important in any business setting.

2. List three characteristics that are part of your polished image.

    a) _____

    b) _____

    c) _____

TOPIC 2: CREATING A PROFESSIONAL ATMOSPHERE

1. Whether you are an employee or self-employed, a _____ room is necessary to function efficiently.

2. Providing a _____ atmosphere is part of your service.

3. Regarding cleanliness and organization, a facility must be _____.

4. Consider the _____ and yours when choosing equipment.

TOPIC 3: FURNITURE, EQUIPMENT, AND ROOM SETUP

1. When setting up a treatment room, think about the _____ you will be performing and how you will _____ at the station.

2. Another consideration is how _____ clients will be while receiving treatments.

3. A basic treatment room should consist of the following basic equipment:

    a) _____
    b) _____
    c) _____
    d) _____
    e) _____
    f) _____
    g) _____
    h) _____
    i) _____
    j) _____
    k) _____

l) _____

m) _____

4. A separate room for mixing products and storing supplies is called a _____.

5. Where should clean items be stored? _____

6. Supplies and products should be kept in _____ containers.

7. The treatment room should be equipped with at least a basic complement of facial supplies. List at least 12 items that should be available to the esthetician.

   a) _____
   b) _____
   c) _____
   d) _____
   e) _____
   f) _____
   g) _____
   h) _____
   i) _____
   j) _____
   k) _____
   l) _____
   m) _____
   n) _____
   o) _____
   p) _____
   q) _____
   r) _____

8. List at least six supplies you should have stocked in your treatment room.

   a) _____
   b) _____
   c) _____
   d) _____
   e) _____
   f) _____
   g) _____
   h) _____

9. List eight basic products that are used in facial procedures.

   a) _____   e) _____
   b) _____   f) _____
   c) _____   g) _____
   d) _____   h) _____

10. To prepare equipment at the start of your workday:

    a) _____
    b) _____
    c) _____

11. Describe the basic steps to prepare the facial bed for a client.

    a) _____

    b) _____

    c) _____

    d) _____

    e) _____

12. List the steps required when setting up supplies:

    a) _____

    b) _____

    c) _____

13. Describe an SMA. _____
    _____

14. The study of adapting work conditions to suit the worker is called _____.

15. When performing a facial, an esthetician's hands should be _____, and feet _____.

16. If prepackaged 4" × 4" esthetic wipes or sponges are not available, cotton pads can be made from a _____.

17. Briefly describe the process for making cleansing pads.

    Step 1: _____

    Step 2: _____

    Step 3: _____

    Step 4: _____

18. What are the two types of eye pads?

    a) _____

    b) _____

19. How do you determine the correct size of eye pad? _____
    _____

20. Summarize the steps in making butterfly eye pads:

    Step 1: _____

    Step 2: _____

    Step 3: _____

Word Review

biohazard	ergonomic	sanitary
bolster	extraction	sharps container
disposable	OSHA	

Rapid Review Test

Date: _____

Rating: _____

Match the following terms with their descriptions below.

covered	client safety	esthetically
biohazard or sharps	closed	state sanitation regulations
butterfly	comfortable/ergonomic	used
contaminated	distilled	vinyl

1. A treatment room should be _____ pleasing.
2. The most important considerations before, during, and after treatment are _____ and _____.
3. To prevent back and hand problems, make sure the work area is set up to be _____.
4. _____ gloves are recommended for use with products containing oils.
5. Unused prepared pads can be stored in a(n) _____ container.
6. _____ pads will not fall from eyes as easily.
7. What type of water is used for the steamer? _____
8. Never store wet brushes in a _____ container.
9. Place soiled disposable items in a _____ container.
10. Proper storage is necessary to keep items from being _____.

TOPIC 4: AFTER THE FACIAL: CLEAN-UP PROCEDURES AND SANITATION

1. List the steps in cleaning and disinfecting implements.

    a) _____

    b) _____

    c) _____

    d) _____

2. List the steps for equipment and room sanitation.

    a) _____

    b) _____

    c) _____

    d) _____

    e) _____

    f) _____

    g) _____

    h) _____

3. Laundry and linens clean-up procedure includes these steps.

   a) _____

   b) _____

   c) _____

4. After the facial, you should dispose of disposable supplies by _____.

5. Disposable extraction lancets and needles go into a biohazard _____.

6. Your end-of-the-day checklist should include these items.

   a) _____
   b) _____
   c) _____
   d) _____
   e) _____
   f) _____
   g) _____
   h) _____
   i) _____

Rapid Review Test

Date: _____

Rating: _____

1. Why is it important to dry off implements before placing in the disinfectant solution? _____

2. Define implements: _____.

3. Clean-up procedures are regulated by _____.

4. A clean, sanitary environment is necessary for _____ and to comply with the laws of the state board _____.

5. Before leaving your treatment room at the end of the day, you should clean anything that has not been cleaned _____.

Activity

Have students make a clean-up check list for between services, and another for the end of the day. Have them inspect the school's treatment rooms to evaluate for neatness, cleanliness, and appropriate organization.

Date: _____

Rating: _____

Text pages: 312–357

CHAPTER 14
Basic Facials

TOPIC 1: FACIAL TREATMENT BENEFITS
1. What is a professional facial designed to do? _____
2. Facials help to maintain the _____ and correct certain _____.
3. Blending a _____ treatment with a _____ experience makes the best overall service.

TOPIC 2: ESTHETICIAN SKILLS AND TECHNIQUES
List eight skills to maintain a client's loyalty.
1. List at least six benefits provided by facial services.
    a) _____
    b) _____
    c) _____
    d) _____
    e) _____
    f) _____
    g) _____
    h) _____
    i) _____
    j) _____
    k) _____
2. For your client to relax, you should speak in a _____ manner.
3. You should always work quietly and _____.
4. Have your supplies arranged in a(n) _____.
5. If your hands are cold, _____ before touching the client.
6. Follow _____ procedures.
7. Be aware of your _____ and the amount of _____ you apply to the face.
8. Never allow _____ to drip down the client's neck, or in the eyes or ears.
9. Massage and remove products in a(n) _____.

TOPIC 3: TREATMENT AND CLIENT PREPARATION
1. One of the most important communications you will have with a client occurs the _____.
2. Always greet new clients by _____, and call returning clients _____.

3. Always approach your client with a _____.
4. _____. Your clients can sense when you are being genuine and open, and they will have more _____ in you and in your expertise.
5. Consider efficiency and _____ costs when determining what to use for draping.
6. Place a towel across the client's _____ and a _____ over the body.
7. List the 11 steps of the facial process.

   a) _____   g) _____
   b) _____   h) _____
   c) _____   i) _____
   d) _____   j) _____
   e) _____   k) _____
   f) _____

TOPIC 4: KEY ELEMENTS OF THE BASIC FACIAL TREATMENT

1. The initial consultation and skin analysis determine the _____ to be used.
2. Before cleansing, you should inspect the skin for the following conditions:

   a) _____
   b) _____
   c) _____
   d) _____
   e) _____
   f) _____

3. You should complete a thorough skin analysis with a magnifying lamp _____.
4. When doing a complete skin analysis, you should note _____ and _____.
5. What are seven contraindications for giving facial treatments?

   a) _____   e) _____
   b) _____   f) _____
   c) _____   g) _____
   d) _____

6. List the steps involved in draping the client's hair with a towel.

   a) _____
   b) _____
   c) _____

7. Products that should be used for lip color removal are _____.
8. When removing lip products, begin with the _____.
9. What three benefits are found in the exfoliation process?

   a) _____
   b) _____
   c) _____

10. Heat applied through steam or warm towels accomplishers what five things?

    a) _____
    b) _____

    c) _____

    d) _____

    e) _____

11. Name the three methods for doing extractions.

    a) _____

    b) _____

    c) _____

12. You must always wear _____ when doing extractions.

13. _____ are metal tools used for open comedones and sebaceous filaments.

14. The skin must be _____ and _____ before extractions.

15. If extractions are done improperly, the follicle walls can rupture and _____.

16. Proper cleansing is essential when extracting blemishes to avoid _____.

17. Once the skin becomes dry and resistive, _____ doing extractions.

18. Identify the areas of the face where the follicles are perpendicular to the surface of the skin:

    a) _____

    b) _____

    c) _____

    d) _____

19. Other areas of the skin, such as the nose and cheeks, have _____.

20. Extractions remove _____ and refine _____.

21. A small, sharp, pointed surgical blade with a double edge is called a _____.

22. Most clients will tolerate approximately _____ minutes of extraction.

23. Describe the proper use of a lancet when opening closed comedones. _____.

24. Describe the benefits of a treatment mask.

    a) _____   d) _____

    b) _____   e) _____

    c) _____   f) _____

25. Depending on their function, masks are applied _____.

26. Toners hydrate and finish the cleansing process by _____.

27. _____ are concentrated ingredients used for specific corrective treatments.

28. Depending on the skin condition, moisturizers can:

    a) _____

    b) _____

    c) _____

29. After finishing a stimulating, nourishing facial, do not send your client out without _____.

30. Antibacterial products and the high-frequency machine kill _____ and help _____.

31. After completing the facial service, quietly and slowly let the client know you are _____.

Word Review

antioxidants	extraction	protocol
benzoyl peroxide	eye pads	serums
capillaries	FDA	skin histology
contraindications	glycolic peel	trauma
debris	hydrate	
exfoliation	lancet	

Rapid Review Test

Date: _____

Rating: _____

Match the following terms with their descriptions below.

contraindications	steps	sanitation
draping	rejuvenate	serums
extractions	remove	time
facial sponges	mini-facial	

1. A facial is a professional service designed to improve and _____ the skin.
2. _____ are conditions that prevent a client from receiving a treatment.
3. _____ the client refers to adjusting the head drape, towels, and linens.
4. Because foam and gel cleansers are harder to _____, it is advisable to use a milky or creamy cleanser that rinses easily during a facial.
5. While cleansing, some estheticians prefer to use wet cotton pads, and others choose to use _____.
6. The skin must be exfoliated and warmed before _____.
7. _____ are concentrated ingredients used for specific treatments.
8. Performing your _____ procedures in your clients' presence will make them feel more confident in you as a professional.
9. The main differences between a _____ and a basic facial are the _____ and number of _____.

TOPIC 5: TREATMENTS FOR DIFFERENT SKIN TYPES AND CONDITIONS

1. Dry skin can appear to be _____ but feel _____ to the touch.
2. Treatment goals are similar for dry and _____ skin.
3. When treating dry skin, use a _____ to exfoliate the face.
4. When treating dry skin, _____ masks can be used.
5. Moisturizing creams with a(n) _____ base are recommended for dry skin types.
6. A skin may have a sufficient amount of oil, but still feel dry and flaky due to _____.
7. When treating dehydrated skin, employ treatments that are similar to the ones for _____ skin.
8. Extreme weight loss can result in loss of _____ and _____.
9. Exposure to extreme climates, too much sun, wind, or polluted air will _____.

10. Mature clients' skin can be improved, but the natural aging process cannot be _____.
11. Treatment goals for mature skin are to _____.
12. When treating mature skin, a _____ will plump and force-feed nutrients into the skin.
13. The primary goal when treating sensitive skin is to _____ the skin.
14. Aloe vera, chamomile, allantoin, azulene, and licorice extracts are all effective on _____ skin.
15. Individuals with sensitive skin should avoid stimulating, drying products and _____.
16. Rosacea, like seborrhea, can be characterized by _____ of the skin.
17. A gentle cleanser, less steam and heat, an enzyme peel, and a soothing gel mask are recommended products/procedures for _____.
18. The best preventive measure for hyperpigmentation is to _____.
19. Brighteners such as kojic acid, mulberry, licorice root, bearberry, and azaleic acid are known to _____.
20. Oily and combination skins need _____ products.
21. Acne facials concentrate on clearing the follicles by _____.
22. Oxygen masks, glycolic acid peels, sulfur masks, anti-inflammatory masks, steaming, extractions, and desincrustation are all treatments recommended for _____.
23. Benzoyl peroxide releases free radical oxygen that kills _____ and sterilizes the _____.
24. Before recommending a salicylic mask, the esthetician must check for _____ allergies.
25. Cleaning out the debris that expands them allows the pores to _____.

Rapid Review Test

Date: _____

Rating: _____

Match the following terms with their descriptions below.

| occlusive | antioxidant | oil | hydration | ampoule | oil-based |
| body | dry | metabolism | natural | physiological | paraffin |

1. _____ products are necessary to protect and balance dry skin.
2. Skin is often _____ dry due to inactivity of the sebaceous glands.
3. The purpose of treatments for dry or mature skin is to stimulate the cell _____.
4. Dry skin requires a(n) _____ cream.
5. _____ skin benefit from collagen, hydrating, paraffin wax, or thermal mask.
6. Dry skin is often due to the _____ aging process.
7. _____ disease, poor health, and psychological problems can cause the skin to appear older.
8. Sodium hyaluronate and sodium PCA enhance _____.
9. Vitamins C and E as well as grapeseed extract have _____ properties.
10. The _____ mask can be applied in a facial or alone.
11. A _____ is used under the mask for specific skin conditions.
12. Melt the paraffin in a warming unit to a little more than _____ temperature.

True or False

1. _____ Hydroquinone is one of many FDA-approved hyperpigmentation treatments.

2. _____ Brighteners such as kojic acid, mulberry, and bearberry are known to reduce pigmentation.

3. _____ In treatments, the suction and the brush machine are too irritating for sensitive skin.

4. _____ Acne treatments may include alpha hydroxy acids, beta hydroxy acids, and sulfur masks.

5. _____ Oil-free products are noncomedogenic.

TOPIC 6: MEN'S SKIN CARE

1. List the key points to consider when choosing skin care products for men.
   a) _____
   b) _____
2. What type of protective clothing do men wear during a treatment? _____
3. Men want a _____ routine.
4. Using the term _____ rather than facial is a better way to promote men's services.
5. Men typically have larger _____ and _____ than women do.
6. Men prefer simple routines and _____ products.
7. When working with men, tubes and pumps are more male-friendly than _____.
8. Cotton pads or gauze will _____. _____ are more appropriate for a man's face.
9. _____ is often referred to as razor bumps.
10. Pseudofolliculitis resembles folliculitis without the _____.

Rapid Review Test

Date: _____

Rating: _____

True or False

1. _____ Professional movements during a man's facial should flow against the hair growth.

2. _____ Men need brisk products so they can feel the results of your services.

3. _____ Pseudofolliculitis is characterized by bumps that are filled with pus.

4. _____ A man's home-care regimen should initially include only two products.

Date: _____

Rating: _____

Text pages: 358–374

CHAPTER 15

Facial Massage

TOPIC 1: THE BENEFITS OF MASSAGE

1. Massage has both _____ and _____ benefits.
2. What four areas of the body is an esthetician's massage limited to?
   a) _____
   b) _____
   c) _____
   d) _____
3. Facial massage has many benefits. List 10 positive results from facial massage.
   a) _____   f) _____
   b) _____   g) _____
   c) _____   h) _____
   d) _____   i) _____
   e) _____   j) _____
4. Hand movements should be _____ and _____ easily from one area to the next.
5. Hand _____ is one way to prevent carpal tunnel syndrome for the technician.
6. What are five conditions of the body or skin that would contraindicate massage?
   a) _____   d) _____
   b) _____   e) _____
   c) _____
7. What care should be taken with the arthritic client? _____
8. List five massage movements used in massage.
   a) _____   d) _____
   b) _____   e) _____
   c) _____
9. The most important movement is _____.
10. Chucking, rolling, and wringing are variations of which movement? _____
11. Generally, massage movements are directed from _____ toward the _____ of the muscle.
12. If it is necessary to remove your hands from the client's face during a massage, you should _____.

TOPIC 2: TYPES OF MASSAGE MOVEMENTS

1. Write the definition of the word in the space provided.

    a) Effleurage: _____

    b) Petrissage: _____

    c) Friction: _____

    d) Tapotement or percussion: _____

    e) Vibration: _____

2. Three variations of friction movements are _____.
3. Where do you use chucking, rolling, and wringing movements? _____
4. _____ effleurage is used on smaller surfaces such as the _____.
5. _____ is a form of acupressure.
6. Friction movement _____ circulation and glandular activity.
7. What movement usually begins and ends a massage sequence? _____
8. _____ is the most stimulating of the general movements, and should be used _____.
9. Describe how slapping movements are performed. _____
10. What part of the hands do you use when executing hacking movements? _____
11. The parts of the body that you use in hacking and slapping movements are the _____, _____, and _____.
12. Vibration is a highly stimulating movement and should never be used for more than a _____ in one spot.

Rapid Review Test

Date: _____

Rating: _____

Match the following terms with their descriptions below.

acupressure	friction	reflexology
aromatherapy	Dr. Jacquet movement	rolling
chucking	lymph drainage massage	vibration
effleurage	petrissage	wringing

1. _____ encourages the removal of waste from the body.
2. A kneading movement that stimulates the underlying tissues is _____.
3. As the hands are working downward, the flesh is twisted against the bones in opposite directions during _____.
4. A technique named after a European dermatologist is _____.
5. A method of applying pressure to points on the body to release muscle tension is _____.
6. Both hands moving at the same time opposite to each other, twisting the flesh up and down the bone, is referred to as _____.

7. _____ is defined as maintaining pressure on the skin while moving the fingers or palms over the underlying structures.

8. _____ is the soft, continuous stroking movement applied with the fingers and palms.

9. When the flesh is grasped in one hand and moved up and down along the bone while the other hand steadies the arm, this technique is called _____.

10. _____ is a technique that is accomplished by rapid muscular contractions in the arms.

11. _____ uses essential oils that penetrate the skin during massage movements.

12. _____ is similar to acupressure; manipulates areas on the hands and feet.

Date: _____

Rating: _____

Text pages: 375–397

CHAPTER 16
Facial Machines

INTRODUCTION

1. The use of electrical devices for therapeutic benefits is called _____.
2. It is important to be aware of current technology to maintain _____ with your clients.
3. Electrical devices are especially effective for more _____ skin conditions.
4. Most machines are used for _____ minutes of the service.

TOPIC 1: SKIN CARE EQUIPMENT

Magnifying Lamp

1. The magnifying lamp is also known as a _____.
2. The magnifying lamp _____ the face to help the esthetician _____ the skin.
3. What type of light bulb is used in the lamp? _____
4. The unit of measure used to indicate the strength of magnification is known as a _____.
5. _____ can be used to protect the client's eyes from the bright light.
6. The lens of the magnifying lamp should be cleaned by _____ and wiping with a _____.

Wood's Lamp

1. The Wood's lamp is a _____ light used to illuminate skin disorders.
2. The Wood's lamp must be used in a totally _____ room.
3. Pigmentation disorders that show up under a Wood's lamp _____ be completely lightened with products or treatments, because the pigmentation is in the _____.
4. Identify the colors associated with the following skin disorders:
   a) Thick corneum layer: _____
   b) Horny layer of dead skin cells: _____
   c) Normal, healthy skin: _____
   d) Dehydrated skin: _____
   e) Oily areas of the face/comedones: _____
   f) Pigmentation problems: _____

Hot Towel Cabinet

1. What items can be warmed in a hot towel cabbie? (towels, cotton pads, and products)
2. Warm towels provide a _____ benefit to the skin and are utilized for removing _____ and _____ the skin before extractions.

3. The inside of the cabbie should be cleaned with a _____ between each client.

4. At night, leave the door _____ to allow the cabinet and the _____ to dry overnight.

Rotary Brush

1. The main purpose of the rotary brush is to lightly _____ the skin.

2. The rotary brush also assists _____.

3. When using a rotary brush on sensitive skin, you should use _____.

4. When using a rotary brush on thicker, oily skin, you should use _____.

5. Brushes should first be washed thoroughly with _____ and then immersed in a _____ _____. When they are completely dry, they can be stored in a _____.

Steamer

1. What are four benefits of using a steamer?

   a) _____ c) _____

   b) _____ d) _____

2. Do not use too much steam on _____ skin.

3. Neglected steamers can become clogged and have a tendency to _____.

4. Steam should be kept approximately _____ inches from the face.

5. _____ are highly active oils and should never be placed directly in the steamer water.

6. What ratio of water and white vinegar should be used to clean the steamer? _____

7. Ordinary oxygen in the atmosphere consists of _____ atoms. Ozone consists of _____ atoms.

8. Ozone has _____ qualities.

Vacuum Machine

1. Never use strong suction, because it may cause _____.

2. Never use suction on _____ skin.

3. Suction stimulates _____.

4. The finger hole on the handpiece should be covered with the index finger when _____.

Galvanic Current

1. Galvanic current is used to create two significant reactions in esthetics: _____.

2. The galvanic machine can leave a _____ taste in the mouth.

3. Galvanic current should not be used when these skin conditions are present: _____.

4. Estheticians use desincrustation or _____ to facilitate deep pore cleansing.

5. To perform desincrustation, an _____-based solution is placed onto the skin's surface.

6. When conducting desincrustation, the client holds the _____ electrode.

7. The chemical reaction that transforms the sebum into soap is called _____.

8. When conducting desincrustation, the electrical current interacts with salts (sodium chloride) in the skin, it creates the chemical _____ or lye.

9. A common desincrustation solution for anaphoresis is _____.

10. _____ is the infusion of a positive product.

11. Most water-based serums can be used as _____ products for cataphoresis.

12. To make proper contact, each electrode must be covered with _____ and the client must hold the _____ pole electrode.

13. List at least eight contraindications for performing a galvanic treatment.
    a) _____
    b) _____
    c) _____
    d) _____
    e) _____
    f) _____
    g) _____
    h) _____
    i) _____
    j) _____
    k) _____
    l) _____
    m) _____

14. _____ is the process of introducing water-soluble products that contain ions into the skin with a(n) _____.

15. _____ are atoms or molecules that carry an electrical charge.

16. Current flows through _____ from the negative to the positive solutions.

17. If the manufacturer indicates that the product is negative, the esthetician infuses the solution with the electrode set at _____.

18. The _____ weight of a product is a factor in permeability.

19. _____ products will penetrate better than oil-based products.

20. An ionto mask facilitates either _____ or _____.

21. When preparing for an ionto mask service, the face is first covered with _____.

High-Frequency Machine

1. The high-frequency machine produces frequency between _____ and _____ hertz.

2. High frequency makes it physically impossible for product _____.

3. Because the high-frequency machine changes polarity 1,000 times per second, it basically has _____ and _____ produce a chemical change.

4. The rapid oscillation created by the high-frequency machine vibrates _____ in the skin.

5. _____ current is used with high frequency.

6. The high-frequency machine provides what six benefits?
    a _____   d) _____
    b) _____ e) _____
    c) _____ f) _____

7. High frequency should not be used on:
   a) _____
   b) _____
   c) _____
   d) _____
   e) _____
   f) _____
   g) _____
   h) _____
8. Clients should avoid contact with _____ during electrical machine treatments.
9. High-frequency machines help _____ and _____ open lesions after extractions by sparking them with the mushroom electrode.
10. True or false: Infrared or ultraviolet rays are used in high-frequency devices. _____
11. How do you clean and disinfect the glass electrode after each use? _____
12. Should the electrodes be placed in an ultraviolet machine or an autoclave? _____

Spray Machine

1. Spray machines are beneficial for _____ the skin.
2. The sprayer can be filled with a _____ solution.
3. When using a sprayer, always place a towel _____ to stop the mist from dripping down the neck.
4. Hold the sprayer approximately _____ away from the face and mist for approximately _____.

Lucas Sprayer

1. The Lucas sprayer is designed to apply the following:
   a) _____
   b) _____
   c) _____
   d) _____
2. The Lucas sprayer is beneficial for _____, _____, and _____ skin types.
3. The Lucas sprayer can be used warm _____ or be used cool for _____ skin.

Paraffin Wax Heater

1. The paraffin wax heater is used to create a warm _____ for hydrating dry skin.
2. Heated paraffin is applied to the face, creating a(n) _____ mask to _____.
3. Always use a _____ wax bath or wax machine that emits a low heat.

Electric Mitts and Boots

1. Boots and mitts apply _____ to the hands and feet to _____ and to _____.

103

2. Boots and mitts perform two important functions: They help _____ and soothe _____.

3. To maintain the electric mitts and boots, wipe them with a _____.

Electric Heat Mask

1. The electric heat mask produces heat at a _____ and is used to help soften the skin for _____.

2. For dry skin, the heat mask is often used in conjunction with a _____, or for _____.

3. For oily, acne, or blemished skin, the heat mask can be used with _____ to soften and liquefy grease deposits.

4. The heat mask is not used on _____ skin.

5. For combination skin with an oily T-zone and areas that are dry, a _____ is applied to the oily areas and a _____ to the dry areas of the skin.

Rapid Review Test

Date: _____

Rating: _____

1. Word Review

paraffin	distortion	therapeutic
diopter	exfoliate	iontophoresis
desincrustation	oxygenate	coagulation
distilled	ozone	saponification

2. Match the following terms with their descriptions below.

spit	pink, red, or orange	white	dehydrated
couperose	15–18	yellow	shape
distilled	oily	sinusoidal	cool
distortion	ozone	antiseptic	

a. Without a clear lens, _____ will add strain to your eyes when using the mag light.

b. A Wood's lamp allows the esthetician to see _____ and _____ areas of the skin.

c. Rotary brushes must be dried in a way that they do not lose their _____.

d. Steamers with _____ have an antiseptic effect on the skin.

e. When steam is used, it should be kept approximately _____ inches from the skin.

f. Mineral deposits cause a steamer to _____ hot water and may cause burns.

g. _____ water is recommended for use in the steamer.

h. Mineral deposit buildup appears as a _____ or _____ crusty film.

i. Lucas sprayers emit a _____ mist, which is beneficial to _____ skin.

j. _____ current is another term for alternating current.

k. Neon gas produces a _____ light.

l. The high-frequency machine has a(n) _____ effect on the skin.

3. What are the two main functions of the vacuum (suction) machine?

   a) _____

   b) _____

4. Vacuuming should not be used on _____ skin.

5. Spray mists are used to _____ and _____ the skin.

6. Should vacuuming be done when distended capillaries are present?

7. The sprayer can be filled with _____ or _____ to refresh and help tone the skin.

Rapid Review Test

Date: _____

Rating: _____

1. Match the following terms with their descriptions below.

anaphoresis	galvanic current	thermolysis
cataphoresis	saponification	sinusoidal
desincrustation	iontophoresis	molecular weight

   a. _____ is the infusion of a negative product during iontophoresis.

   b. _____ uses a positive and negative pole to produce chemical changes.

   c. _____ is the process of using electric current to introduce into the skin water-soluble products that contain ions.

   d. _____ emulsifies or liquefies sebum and debris.

   e. _____ is the chemical reaction that transforms sebum to soap.

   f. _____ is the heat effect used in hair removal.

   g. _____ is infusion of a positive product during iontophoresis.

   h. _____ refers to alternating current.

   i. _____ is a factor in permeability.

2. _____ are atoms or molecules that carry an electrical charge.

3. _____ have greater penetration ability, while _____ cannot penetrate into the skin.

TOPIC 2: PURCHASING EQUIPMENT

1. _____ define which devices are within an esthetician's scope of practice.

2. Make sure the manufacturer's claims about their equipment are _____ and there is _____ to substantiate these claims.

3. _____ and _____ provided by the manufacturer and distributor are two important considerations when purchasing equipment.

4. It may be more affordable to purchase _____ machines rather than the machines that are included in _____ units.

Date: _____

Rating: _____

Text pages: 398–442

CHAPTER 17

Hair Removal

INTRODUCTION

1. The removal of _____ hair is a service offered by most salons.
2. Ancient Egyptians used _____ to rub away hair.
3. The ancient Turks used a crude _____ method for hair removal.
4. Hair removal can represent up to _____ percent of many estheticians' business.
5. Excessive or unwanted hair affects both _____.

TOPIC 1: MORPHOLOGY OF THE HAIR

1. _____ is the study of the hair and its diseases.
2. List the main structures of the hair below the surface:
    a) _____
    b) _____
    c) _____
    d) _____
    e) _____
3. Hair is made from a hard protein called _____.
4. A pilosebaceous follicle is a mass of _____, extending down into the _____, forming a _____.
5. What is the medical term for a hair follicle? _____
6. _____ are slanted, sometimes growing in many different directions in one area.
7. The _____ are attached to the follicle.
8. The lower part of the bulb fits over and covers the _____.
9. Name the areas of the body where no hair grows. _____
10. The papilla is filled with tissue that contains _____ necessary for hair growth and nourishment of the _____.
11. When the arrector pili contracts, it makes the hair _____, causing _____.
12. _____ is the result of activity of the cells found in the basal layer.
13. Hair formation begins _____.
14. The hair on a fetus is known as _____.
15. Very soft, fine hair is called _____.
16. Vellus hair is found on areas not covered by _____ on the _____
    _____.

17. Hair grows an average of _____ per month.
18. What are the three stages of hair growth? _____
19. Which stage produces the most long-term results in terms of hair reduction? _____
20. Hair and skin are the barometers for an individual's _____.
21. Excessive hair growth on the female body suggests a(n) _____.
22. What accounts for how much hair you will normally have on your body? _____
23. What is hirsutism? _____
24. What is hypertrichosis? _____
25. Hair grows faster in a _____ climate.
26. Disease, drug use, and the aging process affect the hair's _____.
27. What hair growth abnormality is often associated with menopause? _____
28. Hair protects the body from _____.
29. Individuals with olive and darker skin tones can have _____ problems if epilation is not performed carefully.
30. Gray hair is _____ and has a deep _____.

Rapid Review Test

Date: _____

Rating: _____

Match the following terms with their descriptions below. The questions may have more than one answer.

arrector pili muscle	hair bulb	lanugo	slanted	root	anagen
bulb	catagen	vitamins	minerals	vellus	dermal papilla
dermal papilla	telogen	trichosis	nutrients		

1. _____: Greek word for hair
2. _____: thick, club-shaped structure that forms the lower part of the hair root
3. Identify the terms that relate to the main parts of the hair follicle. _____
4. _____: inserts into the base of the hair follicle
5. _____: fits into the bulb
6. _____: needed for strong, healthy hair
7. Hair follicles are _____.
8. The terms lanugo and _____ are sometimes used interchangeably.
9. _____: stage in which new hair is produced
10. _____: Final or transition phase.
11. _____: Final, or resting, phase of the hair cycle

TOPIC 2: METHODS OF HAIR REMOVAL

1. Methods of hair removal fall into two general categories: _____.
2. _____ is the process of removing hair by means of electricity.
3. Electrolysis is considered the only _____ hair removal method.

4. What are five popular methods for temporary removal of unwanted hair?

   a) _____

   b) _____

   c) _____

   d) _____

   e) _____

5. Match the definitions with the terminology listed below. (Some words may be used more than once.)

photoepilation	tweezing	temporary hair removal	epilation
thermolysis	blend	galvanic electrolysis	laser hair removal
electrologist	intense pulsed light	depilation	

   a) _____ removes hair for a short period of time.

   b) An _____ is a person trained, licensed, or certified to perform permanent hair removal.

   c) There are three methods of electrolysis: galvanic, _____.

   d) _____ causes chemical decomposition of the hair follicle.

   e) _____ is the removal of hair from the bottom of the follicle.

   f) The _____ method combines the benefits of galvanic and thermolysis methods.

   g) _____ uses intense light to destroy the growth cells of the hair bulb.

   h) _____ and _____ are used to reduce hair growth.

   i) _____ produces a quick flash of light, which destroys the hair bulb.

   j) _____ is the process of removing hair at or near the level of the skin.

   k) _____, waxing, and sugaring are methods of epilation.

6. Barbae folliculitis is the universal technical term for _____.

7. Shaving is a(n) _____ method of hair removal.

8. A _____ is a substance, usually a caustic alkali preparation, used for the _____ removal of unwanted hair by dissolving it at the skin level.

9. Besides shaping eyebrows, tweezing is commonly used on _____.

10. What method or tool transmits radio frequency energy down the hair shaft into the follicle area?
    _____

11. _____ uses cotton threads to lift the hair out of the follicle.

12. _____ is an alternative method of hair removal for clients who are sensitive to waxing.

TOPIC 3: WAXING

1. The primary method of hair removal done by estheticians is _____.

2. Wax is designed to adhere to the _____. When the wax is removed, it removes _____
   _____.

3. Wax that is too hot can cause _____.

4. The skin must be held _____ to avoid skin damage.

5. Name the two types of waxes. _____

6. Waxes may contain different _____ to address the needs of different skin types.

108

7. _____ or _____ may be used for sensitive skin.

8. _____ may be added for its soothing and antiseptic benefits.

9. Hard waxes are considered _____ waxes.

10. Hard waxes are gentle enough to be used on the _____, yet strong enough to remove _____ hairs.

11. _____ have a lower melting point.

12. Strip wax uses a _____ to quickly remove the hair.

13. A multi-tiered, wheeled cart is useful for holding the _____.

14. List the common items you need to perform a waxing service.
    a) _____
    b) _____
    c) _____
    d) _____
    e) _____
    f) _____
    g) _____
    h) _____
    i) _____

15. Tweezers should be made of _____ to avoid corrosion during the disinfecting process.

16. Tweezers with pointed tips are better for removing _____.

17. Slant-tipped tweezers are ideal for _____.

18. Disposable wax applicators are _____.

19. When using strip wax, prepare your strips _____.

20. With correct strip sizes, less material is _____, and more accurate _____ is assured.

21. To keep the waxing area clean, place a _____ for each new client.

22. What is the purpose of applying a prep solution before waxing? _____

23. Products used for ingrown hairs keep the _____.

24. Never _____ the spatula in the waxing pot.

25. List at least 10 skin conditions that prohibit facial waxing.
    a) _____
    b) _____
    c) _____
    d) _____
    e) _____
    f) _____
    g) _____
    h) _____
    i) _____

j) _____

k) _____

l) _____

m) _____

n) _____

26. What two forms should clients either fill out or sign before any waxing service? _____

27. What is the purpose of wearing gloves during waxing services? _____

28. If hair is too long, what should you do before applying the wax? _____

29. Hair must be at least _____ in length for waxing to be effective.

30. Which type of wax has a relatively high incidence of allergic reactions? _____

31. What is the best way to prevent burns? _____

32. Clients should avoid the following for 24 to 48 hours after receiving a waxing service.

   a) _____

   b) _____

   c) _____

   d) _____

33. List the three most important waxing techniques used during the actual wax removal service.

   a) _____

   b) _____

   c) _____

34. What direction is the wax applied? _____

35. What direction is the wax removed (both hard and soft)? _____

36. The natural arch of the eyebrow _____ above the eye socket.

37. When tweezing the hair, pull the hair in the _____.

38. After waxing, dispose of all materials in a _____.

39. After a waxing service, you should sanitize the work area, including _____

40. Men may grow wiry hair on the edge of their ears and on the inside of nose. Should you routinely wax these areas? _____

Rapid Review Test

Date: _____

Rating: _____

Word Review

adhere	hair growth rate	regrowth
skin test	hair texture	shaving
diabetic	heredity	wax pot
electrologist	hirsutism	talcum powder
electrolysis	hormone	tea tree
epilation	hypertrichosis	temporary
fabric strip	lanugo	thermolysis
galvanic	muslin	wax method
growth angle	dermal papilla	
hair growth direction	permanent hair removal	

Match the following terms with their descriptions below.

depilatories	hirsutism	thermolysis
laser and photo light	hypertrichosis	
epilation	permanent	
galvanic	temporary	

1. _____ methods of hair removal destroy or irreparably damage the dermal papilla.
2. The methods of permanent hair reduction by electricity are _____.
3. With _____ methods of hair removal, ongoing treatments are necessary.
4. Waxing and tweezing are examples of _____.
5. Excessive growth of hair where hair does not normally grow is called _____.
6. The presence of excess hair growth on the face, arms, and legs is called _____.
7. The _____ method destroys the hair by decomposing the dermal papilla.
8. The _____ method destroys the hair by coagulating the dermal papilla.
9. A popular group of temporary, chemical hair removers are called _____.

Date: _____

Rating: _____

Text pages: 443–466

CHAPTER 18
Advanced Topics and Treatments

TOPIC 1: PEELS FOR SKIN CARE THERAPISTS

1. In the field of skin care, removing excess accumulations of dead cells on the corneum layers is called _____, _____, _____, and _____.

2. Physicians use peel procedures that are designed to penetrate _____ into the skin.

3. Physicians have used peels since _____ by using these acids: _____

4. The CRF (cell renewal factor) or _____ is the rate of cells _____ and _____ from the dermis to the top of the epidermis.

5. Factors influencing CRF include:

   a) _____

   b) _____

   c) _____

   d) _____

   e) _____

   f) _____

6. The keratinized corneum layer is composed of approximately _____ layers and varies in _____ in different body areas.

7. Over-peeling is _____ to the skin.

8. AHAs are _____ acids.

9. A pH of less than _____ is not recommended for salon glycolic peels.

10. Name several light peels that may be administered by an esthetician.

    a) _____

    b) _____

    c) _____

    d) _____

11. What alphahydroxy acids were originally derived from the following substances?

    a) sugar cane: _____

    b) milk: _____

    c) grapes: _____

    d) apples: _____

12. Salicylic acid has _____ and _____ properties.

13. Peels have many benefits, including:
    a) _____
    b) _____
    c) _____
    d) _____
    e) _____
    f) _____
    g) _____
    h) _____

14. List 10 conditions that restrict the use of peels.
    a) _____
    b) _____
    c) _____
    d) _____
    e) _____
    f) _____
    g) _____
    h) _____
    i) _____
    j) _____

Rapid Review Test

Date: _____

Rating: _____

True or False

1. _____ The average rate of cell turnover for teens occurs in 14 days.

2. _____ Depending on state regulations, some estheticians may use Jessner's solution (1 to 3 coats) to peel the skin.

3. _____ Esthetic peels can remove fine lines and wrinkles.

4. _____ Products with a higher percentage of acid and a lower pH are more irritating.

5. _____ Peels improve the texture of the skin and increase the CRF, hydration, and intercellular lipids.

6. _____ Peels are used to control rosacea.

General Questions
1. What is the purpose of buffering agents? _____
2. How does glycolic acid superficially peel the skin? _____
3. What does the intercellular cement between the skin cells consist of? _____
   _____
4. Name two betahydroxy acids: _____
5. Why does glycolic acid penetrate into the epidermis more effectively than other AHAs? ____
   _____
6. What should you consider when determining whether a series of peels is appropriate for a client?
   _____
   _____
   _____

TOPIC 2: MICRODERMABRASION

1. Microdermabrasion is a form of _____ exfoliation.
2. The microdermabrasion machine is a powerful _____.
3. The vacuum stimulates _____.
4. Microdermabrasion diminishes the following:
   a) _____
   b) _____
   c) _____
   d) _____
   e) _____
   f) _____
5. Briefly, explain the process of microdermabrasion. _____
   _____
6. Improper use of microdermabrasion can cause hyperpigmentation and _____.
7. Microdermabrasion machines consist of the following parts:
   a) _____
   b) _____
   c) _____
   d) _____
8. Carefully clean up crystals while wearing _____.

Rapid Review Test

Date: _____

Rating: _____

1. Match the following terms with their descriptions below:

training	hypopigmentation	vacuum	closed comedones	sun abstinence
complementary	crystal flow	mechanical	couperose	daily sunscreen

   a) Microdermabrasion is a form of _____ exfoliation.
   b) Inappropriate handling of a microdermabrasion machine can cause _____.

c) A series of microdermabrasion treatments should be done in conjunction with _____ products and a complete home-care program.

d) The _____ stimulates cell metabolism.

e) Proper use of the _____, the handpiece, and vacuum setting all contribute to a successful treatment.

f) _____ and certification are absolutely mandatory.

g) Any strong exfoliation procedure requires _____ and _____

h) Microdermabrasion is used to diminish the number of _____.

i) Microdermabrasion is not recommended for _____ skin.

2. List the contraindications for performing a microdermabrasion service:
   a) _____
   b) _____
   c) _____
   d) _____

TOPIC 3: LIGHT THERAPY

1. Lasers use a single _____ at one time.
2. Laser wavelengths are selected to treat a range of _____.
3. Lasers combined with radio frequencies target and heat _____ to stimulate _____ and produce a _____.
4. Light devices that treat the skin via light therapy include _____.
5. LEDs are used at _____ intensity to treat _____.
6. LEDs are likened to _____ by converting light to cellular energy, stimulating the body's collagen and metabolism.

Rapid Review Test

Date: _____

Rating: _____

Word Review

| photosynthesis | alexandrite | intense pulsed light | noninvasive | diode |
| Nd:YAG | laser | radio frequencies | LED | wavelength |

TOPIC 4: MICROCURRENT AND ULTRASOUND TECHNOLOGIES

1. Another term for microcurrent is _____.
2. Microcurrent mimics the way the _____ relays messages to the _____.
3. Microcurrent is regulated according to the _____.
4. What reaction is visible when a microcurrent treatment is performed? _____
5. Microcurrrent is intended to accomplish what four benefits?
   a) _____
   b) _____

c) _____

d) _____

6. Microcurrent devices are designed to work in harmony with the _____ found in the body.

7. Ultrasound and _____ are synonymous terms that refer to a _____ above the range of _____ hearing.

8. The lower the ultrasonic frequency, the higher the _____.

9. Ultrasound in the salon setting is used for reducing the appearance of _____ and enhancing the _____ of products.

10. The _____ damage made by an ultrasound treatment is what _____ collagen production.

11. Ultrasound _____ to assist in product penetration. This is called _____.

Match the following terms with their descriptions below.

faradic	wave therapy	cellulite	collagen	frequency
electrical	ampoule	tissue	medium	oscillations
cancerous	sound	motor nerves	lymphatic	circulation

1. Microcurrent is used to tone the muscles by stimulating _____.

2. Many biological processes are associated with _____ pulses.

3. Microcurrent has largely replaced _____ current.

4. A gel, such as a collagen _____, is placed on the skin before a microcurrent treatment.

5. Microcurrent is also called _____.

6. Microcurrent is reported to aid in the healing and repairing of _____.

7. *Ultrasound* refers to a _____ above the range of _____ that is audible to the human ear.

8. When using an ultrasound device, _____ is affected by the heat manipulation of the tissue and _____ movements.

9. With ultrasound, heat and the vibration in the cells stimulates _____.

10. Ultrasound is based on high-frequency mechanical _____.

11. The heat stimulation created by ultrasound therapies is what stimulates _____ production.

12. Ultrasound vibrations created through a water _____ help cleanse and exfoliate the skin.

13. Contraindications for ultrasound therapy include _____ lesions.

TOPIC 5: SPA BODY TREATMENTS

1. _____ remineralize, hydrate, stimulate, or promote relaxation.

2. Other types of body wraps flush _____ out of the body and promote _____.

3. Body scrubs use _____ to _____.

4. Body masks _____ the body.

5. Hydrotherapy uses water in three forms: _____.

6. List examples of hydrotherapy available in many spas:

a) _____

b) _____

c) _____

d) _____

e) _____
   f) _____
   g) _____
   h) _____
   i) _____
7. Balneotherapy uses _____.
8. Stone massage uses _____.
9. Foot reflexology is the treatment of the body through _____.
10. Ayurvedic concepts are based on three doshas, or _____.
11. Sunless tanning product applications are offered as an alternative to _____.

Rapid Review Test
Date: _____

Rating: _____

Define the following terms.
   1. body scrubs: _____
   2. body masks: _____
   3. reflexology: _____
   4. hydrotherapy: _____
   5. body wraps: _____
   _____

TOPIC 6: MANUAL LYMPH DRAINAGE
   1. Manual lymph drainage stimulates lymph fluid to flow through the _____.
   2. The technique helps to _____ and detoxify the body.
   3. _____ is caused by congestion, water, and waste in the vessels.
   4. _____ is a great addition to a facial.
   5. Manual lymph drainage is used _____ and _____ some surgeries.
   6. _____ is a manual lymph drainage service performed with machines.

Rapid Review Test
Date: _____

Rating: _____

Activity
Have students practice manual lymph drainage on each other. Check for pressure, points of pressure, and results.

TOPIC 7: CELLULITE
1. Cellulite is caused primarily by _____.
2. Cellulite consists of _____.
3. Cellulite is visible when _____.
4. Keeping _____ and _____ healthy helps reduce cellulite.
5. If the epidermis is weakened or dehydrated, _____ is more visible.
6. Repairing _____ damage is important in treating cellulite.

Rapid Review Test
Date: _____
Rating: _____

True or False
1. _____ B vitamins may be beneficial for cellulite reduction.

2. _____ Detox diets, liposuction, and muscle-stimulating systems are cellulite minimizers.

3. _____ Reducing wasted water and preventing free radical damage are part of a healthy approach to treating cellulite and the skin.

4. _____ *Thalassa* is Greek for "sea."

5. _____ Massage cannot help soften hardened cellulite.

TOPIC 8: MEDICAL AESTHETICS
1. Medial aesthetics integrate _____ procedures with esthetic treatments.
2. The most popular medical spa services are:
    a) _____
    b) _____
    c) _____
    d) _____
    e) _____
    f) _____
3. Long-term skin care management programs often combine _____ procedures and _____ treatments.
4. Pre-operative care focuses on _____.
5. The goals of post-op care include _____
   _____.
6. Botox is derived from _____.

7. Botox causes muscle paralysis or diminished movement by _____.
8. _____ are used to fill lines, wrinkles, and other facial imperfections.
9. Dermal fillers will last longer when used in conjunction with _____.
10. There are two types of surgery: _____.
11. Name the correct procedures for the following descriptions of common cosmetic surgical procedures.
    a) _____: surgery that changes the appearance of the nose
    b) _____: face lift
    c) _____: surgery to remove bulging fat pads inside the lower eyelid
    d) _____: removes fat and skin from the upper and lower lids
    e) _____: smoothes wrinkles; collagen remodeling stimulates growth of new collagen in the dermis
    f) _____: uses a mechanical brush to physically remove tissue down to the dermis
    g) TCA or _____ peels: medical peels used for sun damage and wrinkles
    h) _____ peels: the strongest peels; can be toxic
    i) _____: tummy tuck
    j) _____: breast surgery to enlarge or reduce, or to reconstruct breasts
    k) _____: surgical removal of pockets of fat
    l) _____: minimizes varicose veins

Rapid Review Test

Date: _____

Rating: _____

1. Word Review

mammoplasty	dermabrasion	reconstructive
schlerotherapy	liposuction	phenol
Botox®	transconjunctival blepharoplasty	TCA
collagen	nonablative	phototherapy
Restylane®	Radiesse FN®	dermal fillers
polysaccharide	neurotransmitters	rhytidectomy
injectables	nonablative	hyaluronic acid

2. Match the following terms with their descriptions below.

polysaccharide	combination	hyaluronic acid	rhytidectomy	nonablative
postoperative	Radiesse FN®	injectables	neurotransmitters	Restylane®

   a) Hyaluronic acid is a _____ found in the body and connective tissues.
   b) _____ holds up to 1,000 times its weight in water.
   c) _____ is a hyaluronic acid filler.
   d) _____ is a calcium-based filler.
   e) Botox® blocks _____.

    f) _____ means the treatment does not remove tissue.

    g) _____ are nonsurgical procedures.

    h) _____ is the medical name for a face lift.

    i) A medi-spa is the _____ of a medical clinic and spa in one location.

    j) In medical clinics, medical estheticians perform pre- and _____ treatments.

True or False

1. _____ Glycolic peels should not be performed before laser resurfacing.

2. _____ The contraindications for microdermabrasion are more stringent than for peels.

3. _____ Permanent makeup is sometimes performed by estheticians in a clinical setting.

4. _____ Massage, hydration, protection, and camouflage makeup are all part of pre-op care.

5. _____ Postop care includes providing skin care for rapid wound healing.

Date: _____

Rating: _____

Text pages: 467–524

CHAPTER 19

The World of Makeup

INTRODUCTION

1. What is the primary goal of makeup? _____
   _____

2. Different makeup looks can show off an individual's _____.

3. Through the _____, the client's individual needs can be determined.

4. A blend of makeup can enhance a clients's _____.

TOPIC 1: MAKEUP SERVICES OVERVIEW

1. Makeup artists in spas and salons have the opportunity to do:
   a) _____
   b) _____
   c) _____
   d) _____

2. Outside the salon and spa, makeup artists have the opportunity to do:
   a) _____
   b) _____
   c) _____
   d) _____

TOPIC 2: MAKEUP PRODUCTS

1. Choosing a makeup line is similar to choosing a _____.

2. Makeup product choices range from _____ brands to exclusive _____.

3. Advertising costs and overhead costs can affect the _____ of makeup.

Foundations

4. What is the purpose of foundation?
   a) _____
   b) _____
   c) _____

5. Complete the following sentences using these terms:

| cream | oil-free | mineral |
| liquid | powder | |

   a) _____ foundations consist of a powder base mixed with a coloring agent or pigment and are good for oily skin.

   b) _____ foundations are thicker and give medium to heavier coverage.

   c) _____ foundations are suspensions of organic and inorganic pigments in alcohol and water-based solutions.

   d) _____ foundations are water based and are free of mineral oil.

   e) _____ foundations are more noncomedogenic and natural than liquid foundations.

6. What determines the color selection of foundations? _____

7. Which colors denote warm skin tones? _____

8. Which colors denote cool skin tones? _____.

9. When selecting foundation colors, where is the foundation tested to ensure that it will blend well with the client's natural skin color? _____

Concealers

10. Why are concealers used in makeup applications? _____

11. Why is it important to choose the proper concealer color? _____

Face Powders

12. Powders will add a _____ or _____ finish to the face and will help _____ minor discolorations.

13. The two types of powders are _____ and _____.

14. The general purpose of using face powder is to _____.

Blush

15. _____ and _____ are names for cheek color.

16. List two reasons cheek color is used during a makeup application.

   a) _____

   b) _____

17. What specific ingredients are used to make an oil-based cheek color water-resistant?

   a) _____

   b) _____

   c) _____

   d) _____

18. List three different forms of cheek color:

   1. _____

   2. _____

   3. _____

Eye Shadow

19. Eye shadows _____ and _____ the eyes.
20. What is a common mistake when choosing a color of eye shadow? _____
_____
21. A _____ shade will make the natural color of the iris appear lighter.
22. Eye makeup color may match or coordinate with the client's clothing _____.
23. What are the three categories of eye shadow colors?
    a) _____: highlight specific areas
    b) _____: even out skin tones
    c) _____: minimize specific areas and create contour in the eye crease.

Eyeliner; Eyebrow

24. Common forms of eyeliner are _____, _____, and _____.
25. What is the proper procedure for applying powdered eyeliner? _____
_____
26. Most clients prefer eyeliner that is the same color as the _____ for a more natural look.
27. Why is eyebrow color used during a makeup application? _____

Mascara

28. Mascaras are polymer products that contain:
    a) _____
    b) _____
    c) _____
    d) _____
    e) _____
29. What are the inert pigments that give mascara its color?
    a) _____
    b) _____
    c) _____
    d) _____
    e) _____

Lip Color

30. Lip color is available in these forms:
    a) _____
    b) _____
    c) _____
    d) _____
31. When choosing a lip color, what should you take into consideration?
    a) _____
    b) _____

c) _____
d) _____

32. Lip liners are used to keep lip color from _____.

Rapid Review Test

Date: _____

Rating: _____

1. Word Review

corrective	carnauba wax	polymer
lip liner	mineral foundation	contour
mascara	bromic acid	petroleum
diminish	illusion	pigmentation
dramatic	highlighter	film formers
emphasize	inert	thickeners

2. Match the following terms with their descriptions below.

thickening	disposable
sanitized	face shape
concealers	surfactants
darkening	mascara
wipe	defining
demarcation	

a) Natural skin tone, hair and eye color, and _____ should be considered when choosing makeup.

b) A line of _____ should never be visible when applying foundation.

c) _____ should be used sparingly, and _____ on the edges for a natural look.

d) Mascara finishes the eyelashes by _____, _____, and _____ them.

e) _____ enable cream cheek colors to penetrate the hair follicles and cracks of the skin.

f) The pencil sharpener should be _____ after each use to avoid contamination.

g) It is important to _____ the sharpened pencil with a clean tissue to remove loose particles.

h) _____ is a polymer product.

i) _____ wands are used when applying mascara to avoid double-dipping.

TOPIC 3: BRUSHES

1. Makeup brushes may be made of _____ or _____ hair and have wooden or _____ handles.
2. A _____ can be used for quick cleaning.
3. A gentle _____ or _____ is used to thoroughly clean makeup brushes.
4. Brushes must be _____ properly after each client with liquid _____ and a _____.
5. The brush should always be put into water with the _____ pointing downward.
6. When caring for brushes, do not pull on the _____.
7. Carefully _____ your brushes before drying.
8. Cover clean brushes with a _____ and put them in a _____ when dry.

Rapid Review Test

Date: _____

Rating: _____

1. Describe the purposes of the following makeup brushes:
   a) powder brushes: _____
   b) concealer brushes: _____
   c) blush brushes: _____
   d) lip brushes: _____
   e) eye shadow brushes: _____
   f) lash and brow brushes: _____

TOPIC 4: MAKEUP COLOR THEORY

1. _____, _____, and _____ are considered primary colors. What separates these colors from all other colors? _____
2. How are secondary colors created? _____
3. Tertiary colors are obtained by mixing equal amounts of a secondary color with its _____ neighbor.
4. By using a color wheel, create six tertiary colors.
   a) _____
   b) _____
   c) _____
   d) _____
   e) _____
   f) _____
5. How are neutral colors created from primary and secondary colors? _____
6. How do you create a greater contrast between colors? _____
7. Create three scenarios of contrasting colors, using a color wheel.
   a) _____
   b) _____
   c) _____
8. Colors are classified as _____, _____, or cool.
9. Warm tones have which undertones? _____
10. Cool tones have which undertones? _____
11. Which two colors can be considered warm and cool? _____
12. What three factors must you take into consideration when choosing makeup colors?
    a) _____
    b) _____
    c) _____

Rapid Review Test

Date: _____

Rating: _____

True or False

1. _____ Medium skin is always considered neutral.

2. _____ Water-based foundations are noncomedogenic.

3. _____ Foundations that contain mineral oil or other oils are referred to as oil-based foundations.

4. _____ To create dramatic eyes, you should use the same color of eye shadow as the eye color.

5. _____ Light skin can be warm, cool, or neutral.

6. _____ Eye shadow colors are sometimes referred to as bases.

7. _____ Purple eye shadow is ideal for blemished skin.

8. _____ Red will disguise freckles.

9. _____ To avoid a chalky or ghostly look, it is best to use lighter colors.

TOPIC 5: ASSESSING THE CLIENT'S FEATURES

1. The general rule when applying makeup is to _____ the attractive features and _____ the less attractive ones.
2. When determining skin color, you must first decide if the skin is _____.
3. A neutral skin tone is equal amounts of _____, no matter how light or dark the skin color may be.
4. If skin color is light, you can use soft colors for a _____.
5. If skin color is dark, dark colors will be the most _____.
6. If the makeup color is too light, it will turn _____ on the skin.
7. When you begin recommending eye, cheek and lip colors, _____ will always be your safest choice.
8. Orange is a complementary color to _____.
9. List seven common color choices to complement blue eyes.
    a) _____
    b) _____
    c) _____

    d) _____

    e) _____

    f) _____

    g) _____

10. List six colors that are commonly used to complement green eyes.

    a) _____

    d) _____

    b) _____

    e) _____

    c) _____

    f) _____

11. Brown eyes are _____ and can support any color.

12. Charcoal gray is a _____ color; blue-gray is a _____ color.

13. Describe the result of using red or orange on the eyes. _____

14. If warm and cool colors are combined with eye shadow, cheek and lip color, what is the result? _____

15. Hair _____ needs to be taken into account when choosing makeup colors.

16. It is not recommended to mix _____ and _____ shades on the face.

17. List the appropriate steps when choosing a makeup color palette for a client:

    a) _____

    b) _____

    c) _____

    d) _____

    e) _____

    f) _____

18. Blend the foundation _____ so the client's color is consistent from face to neck.

19. Always set your foundation with a _____ to avoid _____.

20. To correct a ruddy complexion, what color of foundation should be used? _____

21. A skin tone that has a yellowish hue requires a _____ based foundation to neutralize the tone.

22. Why is it important to use correct lighting when applying makeup? _____

Analyzing Face Shapes

23. List the eight facial shapes.

    a) _____

    b) _____

    c) _____

    d) _____

    e) _____

    f) _____

    g) _____

    h) _____

24. Match the appropriate facial shapes with the descriptions below.

| square | triangle | round | inverted triangle | heart | diamond | oval |

a) _____: widest at the jawline, tapering up to slightly narrower cheeks and reaching its apex at a narrow forehead
b) _____: a small, pointed chin and narrow jawline, wider at the forehead
c) _____: wide, angular jawline and forehead
d) _____: widest at the cheekbone and usually not much longer than it is wide
e) _____: wide at the temple and forehead areas, tapering down to a narrow chin
f) _____: widest at the cheekbones; has narrow chin and forehead
g) _____: widest at the temple and forehead, tapering down to a curved chin

Rapid Review Test

Date: _____

Rating: _____

Match the following terms with their descriptions below.

medium tones	blue eyes	oval	warm	contrasting
brown eyes	neutral	bright tones	cool	rust
horizontal	width	skin level	matching	plum brown

1. A _____ skin tone contains equal elements of warm and cool.
2. _____ is a cool neutral.
3. Orange is a complementary color for _____.
4. _____ are neutral.
5. If the skin color is medium, _____ will create an understated look.
6. _____ is a brown-based red.
7. A person's _____ is generally categorized as light, medium, or dark.
8. The ideal face shape is _____.
9. If the skin color is dark, _____ will be striking and vivid.
10. When measuring the face, it is divided into three _____ sections.
11. The standard distance between the eyes is the _____ of one eye.
12. When choosing makeup colors, you must determine whether the hair color is _____ or _____.
13. You can bring out the hair color by either _____ or _____ it with the appropriate colors.

TOPIC 6: CORRECTIVE MAKEUP

1. Facial features can be accented with the _____, subdued with the _____, and balanced with the proper _____.
2. A _____ is formed when the product is darker than the skin color.
3. The use of _____ minimizes prominent features so that they are less noticeable.

128

4. Identify the facial features that the following descriptions help correct.

| protruding forehead | wide nose | short nose | double chin | narrow forehead | wide jaw | receding chin |

   a) _____: Apply foundation a shade lighter to the center of the nose.
   b) _____: A lighter shade of foundation is blended onto the tip of the nose and between the eyes.
   c) _____: Apply a darker shade of foundation over the area.
   d) _____: Apply a light foundation along the hairline and blend onto the forehead.
   e) _____: Apply shading under the jawline and chin over the full area.
   f) _____: Highlight the area using a lighter foundation than the one used on the face.
   g) _____: Apply a darker foundation from below the cheekbones and along the jawline.

Eye Shapes

5. Match the appropriate terms with the eye-correction techniques below.

| protruding eyes | hidden lids | small eyes | wide-set eyes | close-set eyes | round eyes | deep-set eyes |

   a) _____: Shadow evenly and lightly across the lid from the edge of the lash line to the crease.
   b) _____: Extend the shadow slightly beyond the eyes.
   c) _____: Blend a dark shadow over the prominent part of the eyelid, carrying it lightly toward the eyebrow.
   d) _____: Apply shadow to the inner side of the eyelid toward the nose and blend.
   e) _____: Lightly apply darker shadow on the outer edge of the eyes and light on the inside near the nose.
   f) _____: Extend the shadow beyond the outer corners of the eyes.
   g) _____: Use bright, light, reflective colors.

Eyebrow Shapes

6. To create a perfect eyebrow shape, you must measure the eyes using these three lines:
   a) _____
   b) _____
   c) _____

7. When correcting an eyebrow shape, begin by _____.

8. When there are spaces in the eyebrow hair, they can be filled in with _____ of an eyebrow pencil.

9. Over-tweezed eyebrows can make the face look _____ or may give the eyes a _____.

10. When the eyebrow arch is too high, remove the superfluous hair from the _____ and fill in lower part with a(n) _____.

11. Making the eyebrows almost straight can create the illusion of a _____.
12. To make the eyes appear farther apart, _____ between the eyebrows and slightly _____.
13. To help correct a round face shape, _____ to make the face appear narrower.
14. A _____ gives more height to a very low forehead.

Lip Shapes

15. When correcting a lip shape, it is best to _____.
16. To correct a thin lower lip, _____.
17. To correct a thin upper lip, _____.
18. To correct a small mouth and lips, use a lip pencil to _____.

Skin Tones

19. The most common skin tones you will be asked to correct are _____.
20. Sallow skin has a _____ hue.
21. Ruddy skin is _____.
22. To correct _____, apply a pink-based foundation.
23. To correct _____, apply a light layer of foundation with a yellow base over the entire complexion.
24. When dealing with ruddy skin, you should avoid using _____ blushes.
25. When dealing with sallow skin, you should avoid using _____ colors for eyes, cheeks, and lips.

Rapid Review Test

Date: _____

Rating: _____

1. Word Review

complementary	illusion	ruddy
contour	incandescent	sallow
cool	inverted	secondary
emphasize	minimize	subdue
enhance	neutral	translucent
fluorescent	pigment	tertiary
harmony	primary	vertical
horizontal	proportional	warm

2. Match the following terms with their descriptions below. (Some terms may be used more than once.)

complementary	triangle	round
diamond	light	shadowing
flat	neutral	square
highlighting	pear	three-fourths
horizontal	pigmentation	
intensity	warm	

a) Colors located directly opposite each other on the color wheel are called _____ colors.

b) Colors are categorized as warm, cool, and _____.

c) Skin color is determined by the amount of _____ in the skin.
d) Dark colors used on _____ skin will create a dramatic look.
e) To emphasize color effectively, it is suggested to use _____ colors.
f) _____ and cool colors mixed on a face create an unbalanced appearance.
g) The face is divided into three _____ sections for the purpose of determining proportions.
h) A _____ face is broader in proportion to its length.
i) A square jawline and wide forehead are characteristics of a _____ face.
j) The ideal face is approximately _____ wide as it is long.
k) A facial shape with a jawline that is wider than the forehead is classified as an _____ or _____ shape.
l) A _____-shaped face is widest at the cheekbones.
m) In makeup, _____ emphasizes while _____ minimizes.
n) It is best to use _____ lip color on large, full lips.

3. On the following diagrams, use colored pencils or crayons to shade the eyes and lips to best enhance or correct the irregularities.

Eye Shapes

Hidden lids

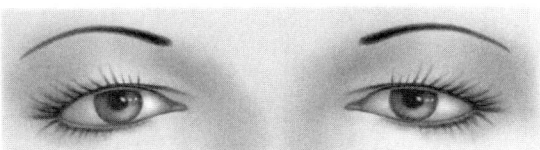

Deep-set eyes

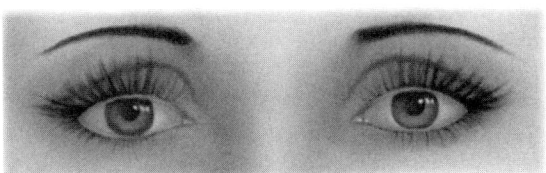

Small eyes

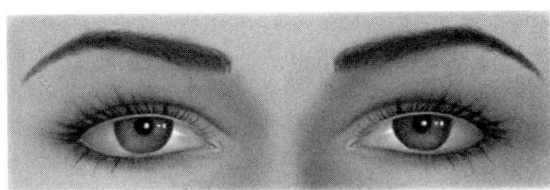

Close-set eyes

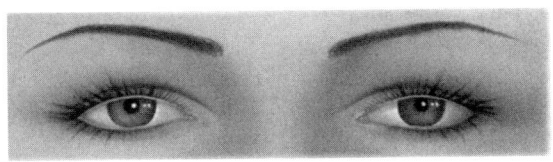

Round eyes

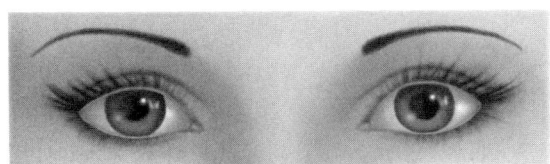

Wide-set eyes

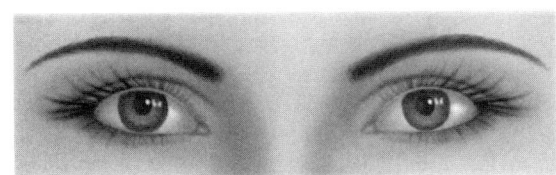

Protruding eyes

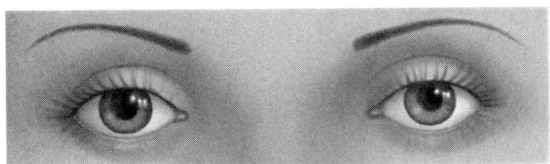

Drooping eyes

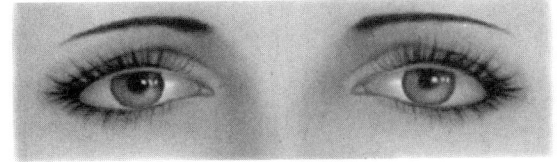

Lip Shapes

Thin lower lip

Thin upper lip

Thin upper and lower lips

Cupid bow or pointed upper lip

Large, full lips

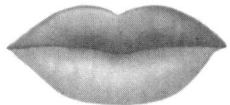

Small mouth and lips

Drooping corners

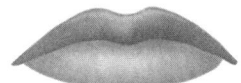

Uneven lips

Straight upper lip

Fine lines around the lips

TOPIC 7: CLIENT CONSULTATIONS

1. The _____ step in the makeup process is the consultation.
2. Have the client _____ to gain insights into her makeup needs.
3. Listen closely to what your client is saying about makeup, and try not to impose _____.
4. During the consultation, specific information should be gathered. List eight elements to be discussed with your client.

   a) _____
   b) _____
   c) _____
   d) _____
   e) _____
   f) _____
   g) _____
   h) _____

5. Record your consultation findings on a _____.
6. Write down the colors you use and note your recommendations on the _____.
7. The area that you use for services and consultations must be _____.
8. _____ and flattering lighting is essential for a makeup application.
9. Make sure the light always shines _____ on the client's face.
10. Clients who see the finished look in _____ are more comfortable with purchasing the products you recommend.

Sanitation

11. _____ off powders before and after application if contaminated.
12. _____ to remove lipstick that you will be using for your application.
13. Use _____ applicators to distribute products.
14. Sharpen and spray _____ to disinfect, and wipe them with a _____.
15. Do not _____ spatulas; this practice is unsanitary.
16. Wash and _____ artist trays, brushes, and mixing cups after each use.

Activity

Create a dialogue to be used during your makeup consultations that includes all of the information you need to deliver a great service. Make sure to use open-ended questions, and not just yes or no answers. Try it on a classmate, and document the conversation to see if you received all of the information necessary for a complete consultation. Create a closure dialogue that includes a retail segment. Retail can be an important part of your income. Practicing while in school will ensure that you have a solid understanding of how to sell.

TOPIC 8: PRODUCTS, TOOLS, AND SUPPLIES

1. To apply foundation and concealer, a _____ is most effective because of its versatility.
2. What should be used to apply mascara? _____
3. _____ can be used for quick fixes or correcting mistakes.
4. Use a _____ wand to dip into the mascara.

5. For straight lashes, a _____ can be used before mascara.
6. Pumping the mascara wand in and out of the mascara tube _____ the mascara.
7. Use _____ for blotting lipstick or powder.
8. Use a _____ or _____ around the client's neck to protect her clothes.
9. What are mixing cups used for? _____
_____.
10. Concealer is usually _____ shades lighter than foundation.
11. Highlighters are lighter than the _____.
12. _____ are darker shades that are used to define the _____ and make features appear _____.
13. Foundations cover the skin to _____ skin tones and mask _____.
14. Most people need a _____ foundation in the summer and a _____ foundation in the winter.
15. Powder sets the _____ and _____ the makeup blending.
16. Eye shadow used with a thin brush dipped in water works as a _____.
17. Put on a lip moisturizer when _____ the makeup application so it can soak in and moisturize before lining the lips.
18. Light-colored lipstick makes lips _____.
19. Lifting the eye skin is not recommended because it will _____
20. Products must be _____ to give the makeup service a professional, finished look.

Rapid Review Test

Date: _____

Rating: _____

True or False

1. _____ Brushes that are designed to blend powder work better than sponge tips or fingers.

2. _____ Busy makeup artists use multiples of the same brushes each day.

3. _____ For straight lashes, an eyelash curler must be used between coats of mascara.

4. _____ Mixing cups are used to hold all manner of product, especially eye shadows and lip color.

5. _____ Concealer must match the skin tone to look natural.

6. _____ Most skin tones have a yellow undertone.

7. _____ Powder is usually applied before the foundation.

8. _____ Lighter-colored lipsticks make the lips appear larger.

9. _____ Metal lash combs are generally better than plastic combs.

10. _____ You will need to have skin care items at the ready when doing a makeup application.

TOPIC 9: SPECIAL-OCCASION MAKEUP

1. During an application for a special event that will be in subdued light, it is important to remember to use more _____ in the application.
2. What are two special effects you might use for a special occasion?
   a) _____
   b) _____
3. If every feature is intensified, the end result will appear _____.
4. Why is it necessary to apply more product for photography and film/video applications? _____
5. What situations require the most exaggerated type of application? _____
6. Bridal makeup should be done as close to the _____ as possible.
7. For bridal makeup, a _____ look is best.
8. Bridal makeup should be applied after the _____.
9. More _____ are generally used for print work.

Makeup Lessons and Camouflage Techniques

10. Lessons teach _____ and introduce _____ to clients.
11. Lessons are beyond _____, which focus on giving clients a new look.
12. For clients with disfiguring scars, and those fresh from facial surgery, it is important to help them look better and thus _____ about themselves.

Activity

Create a list of questions for a bridal consultation. Make a separate schedule for her big day at the salon just before her wedding.

Activity

Pick two or three ads in fashion magazines, and describe what you would use (colors and tools) to create the models' looks.

TOPIC 10: RETAILING

1. _____ cosmetics is a significant part of the business.
2. Most salons pay a commission ranging from _____ percent on every product you retail.
3. One of the biggest challenges women face when purchasing cosmetics is finding the _____.

4. When you start to use specific and _____ language, you will see a great improvement in your selling technique.

5. While retailing is important, always keep a person's _____ in mind.

6. Makeup displays should _____ in retail products.

7. The price of services and products will vary depending on the _____ location of the salon and the client_____.

Activity

Create at least 10 colorful phrases that would entice clients to purchase makeup.

Activity

Evaluate the makeup displays shown in beauty trade magazines. Which ones would help you increase your makeup retail sales?

TOPIC 11: ARTIFICIAL EYELASHES

1. What are the two types of artificial eyelashes?
   _____

2. Clients with _____ and clients who want to enhance their eyes for _____ are most likely to request artificial eyelashes.

3. Name two types of artificial eyelashes that are commonly applied to accentuate the eyes: _____
   _____.

4. When applying artificial eyelashes, keep in mind that some clients may be allergic to the _____.

5. Testing for adhesive sensitivity can be done two ways: _____
   _____.

6. If there is no reaction to a patch test within _____, it is probably safe to proceed with the application.

7. Synthetic fiber eyelashes are made with a permanent curl and do not react to _____
   _____.

8. When removing artificial eyelashes, use _____ saturated with special lotions.

9. The lash base may also be softened by applying a _____ saturated with warm water and a gentle facial cleanser.

10. To remove the lashes start from the _____ corner of the eye.

11. Lash extensions are single _____ hairs that are applied _____ to the client's natural lashes.

12. The application of a full set of lash extensions can take up to _____; partial applications and _____ take less time.

13. Researching the _____ of a particular adhesive is recommended.

Lash Perming

13. Lash perming is the process of _____.

14. _____ are necessary before performing this delicate procedure on clients.

15. Always check with your _____ about the legalities of performing lash services.

Activity

Perform a patch test for adhesive on yourself, and report the results to your class.

Activity

Talk to an esthetician in your area who does eyelash extensions. Prepare a list of questions in advance, such as why the esthetician chose a particular brand, the long-term results, and the potential income growth from this service.

TOPIC 12: PERMANENT COSMETIC MAKEUP

1. Who performs permanent makeup services? _____

2. A thorough training program and _____ experience are necessary to perform these technical services.

3. Permanent makeup is permanent, and there is no _____.

4. Permanent cosmetic procedures involve implanting color into the _____ of the dermal layer.

5. The most popular permanent makeup services are eyeliner and eyebrow tattooing.

6. Permanent makeup services use specialized techniques that are often referred to as:

    a) _____

    b) _____

    c) _____

7. Permanent cosmetics methods include:

    a) _____

    b) _____

    c) _____

    d) _____

ACTIVITY

Contact at least three permanent makeup companies, and ask what kinds of classes they offer to master this popular skill. Compare notes on which companies offer the best education, and report on your findings.

TOPIC 13: AIRBRUSH MAKEUP

1. Airbrush makeup is _____ on the skin.

2. Airbrush makeup has the following benefits:

    a) _____

    b) _____

    c) _____

    d) _____

    e) _____

    f) _____

    g) _____

    h) _____

3. Makeup applications using airbrushing techniques include _____.

Activity

The best way to learn airbrushing techniques is to practice, practice, practice. Apply airbrush makeup to a fellow student or friend, beginning with the foundation and then adding color to the face. To view the difference between traditional and airbrush makeup, apply airbrush makeup to half the face and traditional makeup to the other half.

TOPIC 14: LASH AND BROW TINTING

1. Lash and brow tinting is used to _____.

2. It is important to keep the tint _____ unless requested for the brow area.

3. Any excess color must be removed within _____, or you could have a problem with stains on the skin.

4. Before a lash tint, the skin must be _____.

5. Apply _____ directly next to the area where you are tinting to protect the skin.

Activity

Under the supervision of your instructor, apply a lash and brow tint to a fellow student and then record your results. What formula did you use? How long did the tint last? Was it darker or lighter than you originally envisioned? What factors influenced the longevity of the tint? (Factors can include choice of color, proper mixing of tint, type of daily cleanser used, how often the face and lashes are washed and with what type of cleanser, if the model uses an oil-based eye makeup remover, lifestyle habits, etc.)

Date: _____

Rating: _____

Text pages: 525–569

CHAPTER 20
Career Planning

TOPIC 1: PREPARING FOR LICENSURE

1. Good study habits and _____ during the course of your esthetics program will come in handy when you prepare for your state exam.

2. List at least 10 ways that you can gain control of a test situation.

   a) _____
   b) _____
   c) _____
   d) _____
   e) _____
   f) _____
   g) _____
   h) _____
   i) _____
   j) _____
   k) _____
   l) _____
   m) _____

Deductive Reasoning

3. For an answer to be true, the entire sentence _____.
4. _____ are more likely to be true.
5. When in doubt, look for _____, such as *all, some,* or *none.*
6. Absolutes, such as *always* and *never,* are generally _____.

Multiple-Choice Questions

7. In multiple-choice questions, more than one answer may be true. You need to choose the _____.
8. When two choices are similar, chances are that _____.
9. As you work through the answers, it is possible to find the answer to one question in the _____.

Matching Questions

10. In matching questions, the _____ answer is always available.
11. It may be helpful to _____ answers as you go along.

Essay Questions

12. Essay questions are _____, allowing the tester some leeway in his/her answers.
13. Before writing an essay answer, _____ what you are going to write to ensure you cover all pertinent points.

On Test Day

14. Listen carefully to all _____ given by the examiner.
15. Enter identifying information, such as _____, before beginning the test.
16. Mark any questions that you _____ so you can easily find them later.
17. Save difficult questions, or ones you are _____, for last.

Rapid Review Test

Date: _____

Rating: _____

Match the following terms with their descriptions below.

| grammatical | time management | state licensing exam | deductive reasoning |
| vocabulary lists | active studier | positive attitude | qualifying words |

1. Developing good study habits and practical skills now will help you prepare for the _____.
2. Read content carefully and become an _____.
3. Separate _____ and study these carefully.
4. A good student has good _____ skills.
5. Maintain a _____ that supports passing the test.
6. One technique you should learn for better test results is _____.
7. Watch for _____ clues.
8. When in doubt, look for _____.

True or False

1. _____ Do not ask the examiner questions; he or she may think you are challenging his or her authority.

2. _____ Read all written directions as you take your test.

3. _____ Answer all questions as you go.

4. _____ Check that you have entered all pertinent information correctly.

TOPIC 2: PREPARING FOR EMPLOYMENT

1. To get the best job possible, it is important to showcase your _____.

2. To define your best qualities, you will need to answer two important questions:
   a) _____
   b) _____
3. The Personal Inventory of _____ will help you answer these questions.
4. Traditionally, the field of skin care grew out of the _____.
5. List the type of beauty/medical business, based on the following descriptions:
   a) _____: offers a variety of skin care treatments that may include facial and body treatments, makeup, nail care, massage therapy, and other holistic health practices.
   b) _____: provides a total beauty experience and may offer a combination of other holistic health practices.
   c) _____: focused on maintaining optimal health and may combine a number of holistic, complementary, or alternative health care practices.
   d) _____: integrates a variety of medical aesthetic and surgical procedures, with esthetic skin care treatments and spa services.
   e) _____: all-inclusive spa retreat.
   f) _____: an amenity spa that provides guests with a variety of spa services.
   g) _____: involves leasing a room to provide services independently.

Rapid Review Test

Date: _____

Rating: _____

Short Essay

1. Treatments in the medical spa are mainly focused on clinical procedures. Name at least 10 of these possible treatments. _____
_____
_____

2. Define *booth rental establishments*; describe their business advantages; and indicate where they might be found. _____
_____
_____

TOPIC 3: PREPARING YOUR RESUME

1. A resume provides a summary of your _____ and highlights relevant accomplishments.
2. On average, a potential employer spends about _____ scanning your resume to decide whether to grant an interview.
3. To create a positive reaction, it is a good idea to know as much as possible about the _____ you are targeting and then tailor your resume accordingly.
4. Once you have determined the style and format of resume that is right for your needs, you can begin to address more _____.
5. In general, the information in question 4 should be integrated into a structure that includes:
   a) _____, address, _____, and e-mail address
   b) _____ and objectives
   c) a summary of _____

d) a history of _____ or experience

   e) any _____ that highlight your credentials

6. Rather than providing a detailed account of your duties and responsibilities, it is often a good idea to focus on _____.

7. To be effective, your resume should be:

   a) _____

   b) _____

   c) _____

   d) _____

   e) _____

8. Accentuate any _____ that you have mastered at other jobs.

9. A good way to start organizing the content of your resume is to compile _____ in your possession relating to your education or _____.

The Cover Letter

10. Your cover letter completes the presentation of your _____.

11. Never _____ your cover letter or resume; it must be typed.

12. You may want to prepare a portfolio of _____.

Rapid Review Test

Date: _____

Rating: _____

Match the following terms with their descriptions below.

resume	tailor	audience	credentials	transferable skills
qualifications	salary levels	achievements	honest	

1. The _____ is your ticket to employment.

2. It is a good idea to know as much as possible about the culture you are targeting and _____ your resume accordingly.

3. A resume is meant to highlight your _____.

4. A resume should include your professional _____.

5. A resume should include any achievements that highlight your _____.

6. Consider your _____ and word your resume accordingly.

7. Accentuate any _____ you have mastered at other jobs that can be applied to a new position.

8. Be _____ in the way you present yourself.

9. Avoid making any reference to _____ or requirements.

Short Essay

Describe the documents you should assemble when preparing to write your resume.

_____

_____

_____

_____

TOPIC 4: THE JOB SEARCH

1. Finding the right work environment takes careful _____.
2. Before you accept the first job opportunity that comes along, take time to find out as much as possible about a _____.
3. When searching for a good job fit, ask yourself the following questions:
    a) What is the most important consideration in terms of work _____?
    b) Am I in agreement with the salon's _____?
    c) Do I have any other obligations that may _____ with the demands of a particular situation?
    d) What support will I need to ensure _____?
    e) Are there any causes that I feel _____ about?
4. A _____ is owned by individuals who pay a certain fee to use the company name and are part of a larger organization.
5. _____ afford the owner greater freedom and control in decision making.
6. The _____ appeals to those who appreciate the full spectrum of beauty services and the opportunity to become part of a larger team or network.
7. The _____ offers the opportunity to care for a constantly changing clientele.
8. Before deciding on a setting that is best for you, take the time to visit and _____ a variety of operations.

The Salon Visit or Information Interview

9. One of the best ways to learn about a salon or spa is to request a(n) _____.
10. If you want to solicit additional information directly from employees or clients after an information interview, always _____ from the salon owner _____.
11. After an interview, it is considered proper professional etiquette to send a _____ note.
12. List at least eight ways that you can professionally network.
    a) _____
    b) _____
    c) _____
    d) _____
    e) _____
    f) _____
    g) _____
    h) _____
    i) _____
    j) _____
13. Request a _____ before sending your resume.
14. Each interview is a valuable _____.
15. Keep perfume _____ and your makeup _____.
16. Nails should be _____.
17. When interviewing, expect to be asked questions such as how you feel about _____ retail sales, and your long-term _____ goals and _____.

18. When interviewing, you should always dress _____.
19. Listen respectfully without _____.
20. An interview gives you the opportunity to demonstrate your _____.
21. _____ make critical remarks about previous employers or instructors.
22. Always _____ the interviewer for the opportunity to present your skills.
23. Some questions to consider asking during an interview include: Does the salon provide advanced _____ opportunities? When will the _____ be filled?
    Is there a salon _____ or job description that I can read?
24. It is illegal to ask questions about your _____
_____.

Rapid Review Test

Date: _____

Rating: _____

Match the following terms with their descriptions below.

ethical	franchise	professional	cause	support
independent	information	consent	employment	drug use
dialogue				

1. If you are passionate about a _____, make sure it fits into the culture of the salon.
2. It is critical to find a salon that is willing to _____ your success.
3. Make sure your prospective employer is willing to _____ to your schedule.
4. Some things to consider when searching for the appropriate work situation are benefits, salary, and _____ considerations.
5. A _____ salon is owned by individuals who pay a fee to use the company's name.
6. A small, _____ salon may not offer employee benefits, but it does offer a more intimate space with fewer employees.
7. During an _____ interview, it is appropriate to ask what customer service policies the manager believes are critical to operating a successful salon.
8. The first step toward gaining a(n) _____ interview is sending in your resume.
9. Presenting a _____ image is critical during your employment interview.
10. During an employment interview, you should create as much _____ as possible.
11. Employers may ask you about any _____.

TOPIC 5: ON THE JOB

1. When you make the transition from student to employee, be aware that a salon will expect you to conform to a _____.
2. As a licensed esthetician, your work revolves around _____.
3. _____ shows clients that you value and respect their time.
4. False claims damage the client's _____.
5. Make sure you are knowledgeable about the _____ you perform and the _____ you use.
6. The main goal of a salon or spa is to _____. As such, keeping a schedule that benefits the salon's clients will become a _____.

7. Performing whatever services and functions your job requires, regardless of personal circumstances, is an _____ of the working world.
8. Understand what your boss expects of you, and work hard to _____.
9. Be willing to share _____ with others.
10. For a salon to be successful, _____.
11. When you encourage and support your teammates to do their best, _____.
12. Rules and guidelines help us to maintain a _____ existence.
13. Successful businesses recognize the need for clear _____.
14. Many companies incorporate a _____ or philosophy in their company manual.
15. A salon may dictate exactly how a _____ should be performed.
16. To ensure the safety of your clients, and to protect yourself and your employer from liability issues, always take a complete _____ before beginning any new procedure.
17. As a general rule, when in doubt, _____.
18. Have clients sign a _____ each time they undergo a procedure.
19. Should a problem arise, inform your _____ immediately and _____ the incident.

Rapid Review Test

Date: _____

Rating: _____

Match the following terms with their descriptions below.

| rules | sales | analyze | organizational | work habits |
| reactions | evaluation | responsibilities | consent form | expertise |

1. Be ready, willing, and able to accept additional _____ whenever necessary.
2. It is an employee's responsibility to understand the _____ of a salon.
3. If you are working for a large organization, the manual may include an _____ chart.
4. _____ to cosmetic products are commonplace.
5. Review the _____ before beginning the procedure.
6. Your duties could include participating in _____ events.
7. Most salons use computerized systems to _____ sales and services.
8. The _____ process provides important feedback for both the employer and employee.
9. Clients need to know they can rely on your _____.
10. Maintaining good _____ will foster success—both for you and the salon.

TOPIC 6: THE JOB DESCRIPTION/EMPLOYEE EVALUATION

1. The job description is an important tool that helps employees to _____.
2. To carry out your responsibilities to the best of your ability, you should be given a _____.
3. Job descriptions are varied according to the _____ and are based on the _____.
4. The number of employees may also affect the _____.
5. Some salons and spas may incorporate other objectives in their job descriptions, such as attitudes that are expected and opportunities for _____.

6. Developing a process for measuring an employee's progress is critical to setting _____.

7. During an employee evaluation, it is helpful to ask your employer for suggestions that will help you to do your _____.

8. In general, estheticians first starting out should expect to be evaluated _____ after they are hired.

9. Understanding your productivity and client satisfaction levels can validate those things that you are doing _____ and provide additional incentive for _____.

10. Employers generally appreciate personnel who are _____ in assuming responsibility for _____.

Rapid Review Test

Date: _____

Rating: _____

Short Essay

During an employee evaluation, you should ask employers what you can do to become more valuable to the salon. Create a short scenario of an employee–employer interview by responding to the following employer observations in a proactive manner:

1. "Your retail sales are still not on a par with our expectations. What do you think you should do to improve this situation?" _____

2. "Have you noticed how our veteran estheticians always come in early to prepare for their first clients? I've observed you coming through the door with your client on several occasions. What do you think about that?" _____

3. "You're really applying yourself, and your clients are appreciating your efforts. What I would like to see, though, is better productivity. You're booking 1 hour 15 minutes for a facial, when my seasoned staff does the same service in 50 minutes." _____

TOPIC 7: COMPENSATION

1. Just as the bottom line for salons is making money, _____ is the primary incentive for estheticians.

2. _____ can be based on either a flat or hourly rate.

3. If you are offered a set salary, it must be at least equal to _____; you are also entitled to _____ if you work more than _____ hours per week.

4. Commission-based wages are directly related to your _____.

5. Many owners are now establishing _____ and implementing tiered schedules to motivate staff to increase their income.

6. Others are implementing a fixed _____ or flat _____ for each service.

7. Many salons are also using a combination of _____ and _____ structures. These include a _____ salary plus commission on products and/or _____.

8. Like restaurants, _____ are customary to express appreciation for a satisfactory esthetics service.

9. Not all salons allow _____, because the IRS considers tips income and employers must pay employee-related taxes on them.
10. Most gratuities range from _____ percent.

Rapid Review Test

Date: _____

Rating: _____

1. Figure out your gross pay (before taxes) on the following service revenues and pay methods:

    $500 gross revenues, 50% commission = _____

    $500 gross revenues, $250 salary + 20% commission = _____

    $500 gross revenues, $300 salary + 20% commission on all revenues over $300 = _____

    $500 gross revenues, $350 salary = _____

    $750 gross revenues, 50% commission = _____

    $750 gross revenues, $250 salary + 20% commission = _____

    $750 gross revenues, $300 salary + 20% commission on all revenues over $300 = _____

    $750 gross revenues, $350 salary = _____

TOPIC 8: MANAGING MONEY

1. Creating a _____ will help you meet your financial obligations.
2. Keeping track of where your money goes is the first step in _____.
3. Once you understand the amount of money you have coming _____, you can make critical choices about your _____.
4. If you find it difficult to manage money, it may be helpful to seek _____.

Activity

To figure out exactly what you must earn after graduating from beauty school, create a personal budget. To do this, add up your monthly credit obligations; insurance costs; overhead such as rent and utilities; the amount you need for gas and groceries; spending money; wardrobe budget; and the money you need to set aside in case of emergencies, such as car repairs. Add it all up and add at least a 15 percent cushion for inflation, etc. Keep this figure in mind when casting your net for an esthetics position.

TOPIC 9: FINDING THE RIGHT ROLE MODELS/CONTINUING YOUR EDUCATION

1. A role model is a person whose behavior and success you would like to _____.
2. A role model can be a more experienced _____ or boss.
3. The world is full of positive _____.
4. Success does not always come to you; you need to make it _____.
5. To keep up with consumer demands and job requirements, estheticians must seek out _____ _____ once they have graduated.
6. Subscribing to trade publications and professional newsletters will help you keep up with _____ _____ on a regular basis.
7. _____ are a good source of education about new products and techniques, although you must keep in mind that they have _____ interests in their products.

8. To learn more about management, or operating your own business, enroll in _____ _____ at a community college or adult night school.

9. Estheticians who are committed to success understand that _____ for advancing their education is ultimately worth the _____.

Activity

Find the show calendars and news about events in trade magazines (printed versions and on the Internet). Contact favorite manufacturers and ask for their class schedules. Use this information to create your own education/show calendar. Mark the events/classes you plan to attend.

TOPIC 10: PLANNING YOUR SUCCESS

1. Successful people are _____ or driven to achieve their _____.
2. Achieving your goals requires discipline and, at times, a great deal of _____.
3. Success is not something that happens _____.
4. Success requires _____ and _____.
5. Be clear about what you stand for, and remain _____ in your dealings _____.
6. Be _____ to yourself.
7. Believe in _____.

Activity

Write down the things that you believe about yourself, and list your self-doubts. For every positive thing you write, provide examples. For every negative thing you write, provide a possible solution to boosting your self-esteem.

Date: _____

Rating: _____

Text pages: 570–598

CHAPTER 21

The Skin Care Business

TOPIC 1: GOING INTO BUSINESS FOR YOURSELF

1. To be successful, you will need to have lots of _____, a clear _____, and solid _____.

2. _____ allows you to experience operating a business on a much _____.

3. Renting space does not necessarily mean that you have complete control over your _____.

4. As a booth renter, you are responsible for paying all personal taxes associated with being _____.

5. Before renting a treatment room, you should find out the rate of turnover of both _____.

6. Some state boards require a special _____ for booth rentals.

7. If you are interested in attracting a high-end clientele, you should seek out a _____ area.

8. High-traffic areas provide access to a larger number of _____.

9. The _____ provides the practitioner with a strategy for understanding key elements in developing a business.

10. Before signing a lease, you should conduct a complete and thorough _____ of what other businesses are offering and the prices they are charging.

11. Hiring a professional business consultant may ultimately be the most _____ way to start up your business.

12. Your business plan should include the following:

   a) _____
   b) _____
   c) _____
   d) _____
   e) _____
   f) _____
   g) _____

13. Learning to think in terms of _____, and profits can help you to gain a more global perspective of business functions as you develop your plan.

14. _____ are constant costs.

15. _____ refer to expenses that can fluctuate.

16. _____ is the money coming in.

17. _____ is the amount of money available after all expenses are subtracted from all revenues.

18. Your business must be in compliance with all _____ regulations.

19. The federal government oversees laws regarding _____ taxes.

20. Although insurance may provide the business owner with a certain peace of mind, it may not protect you from _____ conduct.

21. A salon can be owned and operated by a(n) _____.

22. _____ is one of the best ways that a business owner can protect his or her assets.

23. Corporations are managed by a _____.

24. Should you decide to purchase an established salon, always seek the professional advice of a(n) _____ and _____.

25. When renting or leasing space, be prepared to _____ of your agreement with your landlord.

26. To operate a successful salon, you will need a variety of _____ and _____ skills.

27. The smart businessperson recognizes that she or he _____ be all things.

28. Working from your business plan, determine how much _____ you will need to operate your business for at least two years.

29. Before you can determine the price for _____ and _____, you need to understand their value.

30. Proper service pricing begins with exact knowledge of what it costs to provide each _____.

31. To stay in business, you must learn to work _____ with your staff.

32. To attract quality and experienced help, you must be willing to offer _____ salaries and benefits.

33. The well-run salon offers _____ policies and posts these in an area that is _____.

Rapid Review Test

Date: _____

Rating: _____

1. Match the following terms with their descriptions below.

day-to-day	liability	apprenticeship	functions	malpractice
treatments	parameters	strategic	visibility	accessibility

   a) Booth rentals allow the esthetician to operate a business within certain _____.

   b) A booth renter is responsible for conducting all necessary business _____.

   c) Some states require estheticians to complete a(n) _____ before becoming a booth renter.

   d) In a booth rental situation, being the sole person responsible for all _____ operations is a big responsibility.

   e) As a booth renter, you will be required to procure _____ and _____ insurance.

   f) Determining the types of _____ you want to offer will help you to define your business.

   g) Once you are clear about your overall business concept, you are ready to develop a _____ plan.

   h) Once you have defined your target market, you can address factors such as _____ and _____.

2. True or False

   a) _____ One of the most crucial elements in attracting business is parking.

   b) _____ It is usually in your best interest to locate your salon in a high-density, high-competition area.

   c) _____ It is a wise idea to develop a unique menu of services.

   d) _____ One of the best ways to find your target market is to study the area's demographics.

   e) _____ A business plan will help you afford the things you will need for your business.

3. Match the following terms with their descriptions below.

revenue	variable	capital	accountant	corporation
profit	sole proprietor	fixed	remain	initial

   a) _____ is the money available after meeting all financial obligations.
   b) _____ costs refer to expenses such as utilities, supplies, and advertising.
   c) _____ is the income generated from selling services and products.
   d) _____ costs refer to expenses such as rent and loan payments.
   e) A _____ is accountable for all expenses and receives all profits.
   f) One advantage to having a partnership is increased _____.
   g) In a _____, taxation is limited to the salary that you draw.
   h) Most buyers are concerned about the _____ return on their investment.
   i) Before buying an existing salon, seek the advice of a(n) _____ and business lawyer.
   j) When purchasing an existing salon, it is important to ascertain that the existing employees will _____ with the salon.

4. In general, a purchase agreement to buy an established salon should include:

   a) a formal written and _____ purchase and sale agreement.
   b) a complete and signed statement of _____, including all products, equipment, and fixtures.
   c) free and _____ use of the salon's name.
   d) complete _____ of all information.

5. When renting or leasing space, be prepared to _____ the terms of your agreement with your landlord.

6. When writing up a lease, allow a(n) _____ for fixtures or appliances that are attached to the salon so they can be removed without violating the lease.

7. Include the option that you can _____ your salon to another person.

8. It can be helpful to create a _____ for closing or opening the salon.

9. In general, the type of salon and clientele it serves determines the cost of _____ and _____.

TOPIC 2: THE IMPORTANCE OF KEEPING GOOD RECORDS

1. Keeping accurate track of daily, weekly, and monthly records will help you to determine _____ _____.
2. Income is generally recorded as _____ from sales and services.
3. Do not forget to document any miscellaneous or cash expenses for _____ reporting purposes.
4. Small cash outlays may be kept in a _____ notebook.
5. Understanding the amount and types of services that are performed can serve as a _____ and _____ system for using products and controlling expenses.
6. Inventory can be broken down into two categories: _____.
7. Inventory and purchase records will help to prevent _____ and avoid _____.
8. Client records are instrumental in _____ the overall performance of the salon or _____.
9. Understanding what _____ and _____ clients need or want will ultimately increase sales and improve client _____.
10. In today's impersonal world, the simplest _____ can make a significant difference in how the client _____ your efforts.

Rapid Review Test

Date: _____

Rating: _____

Match the following terms with their descriptions below.

net worth	financial	manual	conducting	marketing
trends	retail supplies	tracking	correctly	objectives

1. You will need to keep good records to manage your accounts efficiently and _____.
2. A bookkeeper is trained in _____ record keeping.
3. Keeping track of daily, weekly, and monthly records is useful in assessing the _____ of your business.
4. Whether you choose a computerized program or _____ method, you will need to keep track of all sales on a daily basis.
5. _____ inventory and supplies are important parts of _____ business.
6. Accurate records can help you to determine which _____ are sold most often.
7. Analyzing accurate client records provides useful information for tracking customer _____ and performing _____ tasks.
8. Maintaining accurate client records allows you to meet your business _____, including customer service and performance analysis.

TOPIC 3: OPERATING A SUCCESSFUL SKIN CARE BUSINESS

1. The one thing that most salon owners have in common is the willingness to _____.
2. Even though luck might play a role in business success, without a great deal of _____ _____, and continued hard work, most businesses will ultimately fail.
3. A business plan will help you to stay on _____ and within _____ as you make all the necessary decisions and purchases associated with operating your salon.
4. The _____ and _____ of both clients and practitioners should be primary concerns when _____ the treatment room.

5. When physically laying out your salon, you should ask yourself these questions:
   a) Is the color scheme one that is inviting to a _____ of clients?
   b) Does the style of the salon evoke a professional ambiance that instills client _____?
   c. Is aisle space adequate for safety and _____?
   d) Does your dispensary have _____ and ease of mobility?
   e) Are restrooms easily _____?
   f) Do air conditioning and heating systems supply adequate _____ and temperature _____?
6. Searching for good employees can be _____.
7. To maximize your efforts in finding good employees, develop a list of _____ and _____ for evaluating prospective employees.
8. For some salons, the opportunity to increase _____ is a prerequisite for employment.
9. Training new staff takes _____ and _____.
10. Efficiently run salons provide employees with clear _____.
11. A _____ is extremely useful in helping employees understand what is expected of them.
12. A _____ can provide a reasonable standard for evaluating an employee's performance.
13. The _____ may cover general information about the salon operations, such as the number of sick days.
14. A _____ is designed to standardize operations and may include specifics about certain services.
15. Treat employees with _____ and _____.
16. Practice _____ communication skills.
17. Set clear _____ and _____, and be consistent.
18. Evaluate productivity, and furnish _____ increases fairly.
19. To become a good manager, you will need a variety of _____ and communication skills.
20. Learn to provide feedback in a truthful and _____ manner.
21. When issues and differences arise, address them _____.
22. Before jumping to a negative conclusion, give your employees the _____ and listen to all the facts.
23. The reception area provides clients with the all-important _____ of your salon.
24. To ensure that clients feel confident when they walk through your doors, you must create a sense of _____ and organization.
25. The reception area is the _____.
26. The receptionist performs a variety of tasks that are critical to maintaining the _____.
27. It is the receptionist's job to _____ good will, instill client _____, and assure customer _____.
28. Staying on schedule is critical to the _____ and _____ of operations and ultimately promotes customer _____.
29. To ensure clarity, it is helpful to identify the specific _____ that should be used when answering calls.
30. Answer calls _____ and return messages _____.
31. Make business calls at a _____ time.

32. Handle price objections or complaints with _____ and tact.
33. Confirm appointments _____ hours in advance.
34. When leaving messages, always address the client by _____.

Rapid Review Test

Date: _____

Rating: _____

1. Match the following terms with their descriptions below.

construction	planning	ethical	modifications	criteria
fair	appreciate	user-friendly	sensible	equitable

   a) Certain design components of your salon may require specific _____.
   b) You should refer to your business plan often during the various stages of _____.
   c) Your business plan will serve as a useful tool throughout the _____ process.
   d) Creating an efficient and _____ workspace requires careful planning.
   e) You will want to establish _____ rules and directions.
   f) Develop _____ and _____ employee practices.
   g) Let employees know that you _____ them.
   h) Establishing set _____ for pay increases sets the tone for a fair and _____ system.

2. True or False

   a) _____ Always keeping your word will instill trust.

   b) _____ A receptionist's job is limited to greeting clients and keeping the salon running smoothly.

   c) _____ The receptionist should be prepared to provide clients with concise and courteous information.

   d) _____ Clients always have a right to book with the technician of their choice.

   e) _____ The Internet is replacing the telephone as the number one method for booking appointments.

3. List at least five guidelines for using the telephone effectively:
   a) _____
   b) _____
   c) _____
   d) _____
   e) _____
   f) _____
   g) _____

TOPIC 4: PUBLIC RELATIONS

1. _____ is a significant factor in building your business.
2. Public relations is all about _____ and _____ relationships to achieve a certain desired behavior.
3. To maintain productive relations and positive outcomes, you will need to work on developing effective _____ and _____ skills.

Rapid Review Test

Date: _____

Rating: _____

Short Essay

Define public relations.

_____
_____
_____

Date: _____

Rating: _____

Text pages: 599–616

CHAPTER 22
Selling Products and Services

TOPIC 1: SELLING IN THE SKIN CARE SALON

1. Selling products and services is critical to the _____ success of a skin care salon.
2. Selling products and services is a fundamental _____ in the skin care business.
3. To frame the concept of sales in a positive light, estheticians must understand that it is their _____ _____ responsibility to recommend products.
4. To successfully sell products and services, you must be motivated and committed to _____.
5. Looking the part, and practicing your own philosophies, are good ways to advertise the benefits of _____.
6. Because you are an expert on skin care, clients place their trust in your _____.
7. When clients rely on your guidance in recommending the best treatments and products for their needs, you are practicing _____ selling.
8. Some clients respond best to a _____ approach that involves recommending which products are best for them without stressing the sale.
9. _____ focuses emphatically on why a client should buy the product.
10. When recommending products, you should focus on the client's _____ and _____.
11. You should close the sale without over-_____.
12. In the relationship between _____ and _____, there must be a balance between what the client wants and what the professional knows is in the client's _____.

Rapid Review Test
Date: _____
Rating: _____

Match the following terms with their descriptions below.

connotations	consultative	principles	false	sensitively
personalities	practicing	productive	intelligence	accommodate

1. If a client does not realize that her current skin care program is not in her best interest, it is your obligation to _____ let her know why this is so.
2. Respect clients' _____ and acknowledge their efforts to advocate for themselves.

3. To move beyond the negative _____ of selling, estheticians must learn to recognize the value of selling.

4. Once you have accepted selling as a necessary and reputable part of your job, you can begin to work on developing _____ that promote ethical sales practices.

5. It is your job to help clients resolve skin care issues in the most _____ way.

6. Looking the part and _____ your own philosophies is a good way to advertise the benefits of healthy skin care.

7. When providing guidance about skin care, recommending skin care products is known as _____ selling.

8. Never make _____ or unrealistic claims.

9. You will encounter many different _____ with various skin care concerns.

10. Adjusting your sales technique to _____ the client's style is a technique that will help you to sell in a professional manner.

TOPIC 2: KNOW YOUR PRODUCTS AND SERVICES

1. Increasing your _____ makes it easier to educate clients and increase _____.

2. _____ is the act of recommending and _____ products to clients for at-home use.

3. Estheticians should develop a _____ knowledge of _____ and the effects they have on skin.

4. Breaking down _____ into more manageable categories is a good way to begin sorting through the overwhelming amount of information about products that exists today.

5. Once you have defined a company's _____, you should assess the quality of its products and methods of _____ and _____.

6. Learning firsthand about the results experienced by other skin care professionals is a good way to _____ of a product.

7. Look for companies that supply a simple format to explain the _____ and _____ of a product.

8. The following points should be kept in mind when selling:

    a) Establish _____ with the client.

    b) Determine the client's _____.

    c) Recommend _____ and _____ based upon those needs.

    d) Emphasize _____.

    e) Close the _____.

9. The best marketing materials and educational support are not substitutes for your _____.

10. The _____ supplies the esthetician with valuable information about the client's skin care habits and goals.

11. The questionnaire or _____ is an important tool that allows the esthetician to learn about the overall skin condition of a client.

12. _____ refers to a method of taking personal notes that help the esthetician serve the client's needs better.

157

13. Before you inundate the client with a lot of detailed information, find out what the client _____ _____ about her or his skin.
14. Be honest about what you do not _____.

Rapid Review Test

Date: _____

Rating: _____

Match the following terms with their descriptions below.

| recommending | motivation | knowledge | seminars | believe |
| intimidated | confidence | demonstrate | up-selling | educate |

1. Whenever possible, _____ the use of products and treatments.
2. It takes time to develop _____ in recommending products.
3. The novice esthetician can be easily _____.
4. Increased _____ makes it easier to educate clients and boost retail sales.
5. Understanding the consumer's _____ for purchasing products will help you to refine your sales approach.
6. Because you are the expert on skin care, clients will rightfully assume you are _____ the right products for their skin care needs.
7. Many manufacturers and distributors offer _____ to attract new business and to _____ professionals about their products.
8. To successfully sell products, you must first _____ in yourself.
9. _____ is the practice of recommending additional services or products to clients.

TOPIC 3: MARKETING

1. _____ provides a strategy for how goods and services are bought and sold, or exchanged.
2. Marketing is more than a sales _____.
3. To successfully market skin care products and services, you must recognize that marketing serves both the _____ and _____.
4. All marketing programs involve some form of _____.
5. A _____ is aimed at getting the customer's attention with the goal of increasing business.
6. Marketing includes using seasonal _____ to promote packages at special prices.
7. Estheticians should endorse their salon's _____-buyer programs, or _____ savings discounts.
8. Introduce new customers to services with a special _____ offer.
9. Offer _____ to add value to services on slower days.
10. _____ encompasses any activity that favorably promotes the salon or spa.
11. _____ typically refers to promotional efforts that are paid for, and they are directly intended to increase business.
12. Advertising helps build _____ by increasing _____.

Rapid Review Test

Date: _____

Rating: _____

1. _____ provides a strategy for how goods and services are bought and sold.
2. Promotion methods include:
   a) _____
   b) _____
   c) _____
   d) _____
   e) _____
   f) _____
3. Introduce new products with _____ samples.
4. _____ is any activity that promotes the salon favorably.
5. The best form of advertising is a _____ customer.
6. A good esthetician takes advantage of advertising by being knowledgeable about _____ and bringing them to the attention of clients.

TOPIC 4: BUILDING A CLIENTELE; CLIENT RETENTION

1. A client's initial visit should be considered the salon's first opportunity to make a _____.
2. The successful salon owner knows that _____ clients keep the business going.
3. Developing a bond with clients has a great deal to do with whether they will _____.
4. Clients must have two good reasons for returning to the salon:
   a) The client must be _____ with the treatment and results.
   b) He or she must have _____ in the professional's expertise.
5. Never forget that each client has a _____ agenda.
6. Always set aside time to update information and address _____ concerns.
7. There is no substitute for the genuine respect that comes from _____ to another person.
8. Give your clients _____ to rebook appointments.
9. To keep clients satisfied and loyal, the esthetician must continually provide _____.
10. Marketing-savvy salon owners know that word of mouth is one of the best forms of _____.
11. Getting involved in the _____, and generating positive publicity, are good ways to inform the _____ about your services.
12. The _____ gives the esthetician and the client a valuable opportunity to review client concerns and recommend an appropriate _____ program.
13. When consulting, estheticians must _____ their recommendations clearly.
14. It is the esthetician's job to _____ and _____ clients and provide them with an individual program that they can follow on a _____.
15. A _____ memo summarizes product recommendations and explains proper _____.
16. Once the esthetician has earned the client's trust, she will need to work hard to _____.

Rapid Review Test

Date: _____

Rating: _____

1. After winning over a customer, it is easy to become complacent. To avoid this common pitfall, estheticians must _____.
2. Always set aside time to update information and address client concerns. This lets clients know that you are genuinely interested in _____ their individual skin care needs.
3. Give each client your personal undivided attention. Get in the habit of treating clients like _____ _____.
4. A professional, yet friendly and confidential manner will encourage clients _____ _____. This will enable estheticians to provide a more _____.
5. Current clients are always a _____ of referrals and one of the best methods of _____ for a salon.
6. Many salons implement _____ to purposely encourage client referrals.

TOPIC 5: CLOSING THE SALE

1. One of the most important parts of the esthetician's job actually occurs _____ _____.
2. The closing consultation is a time to _____ clients about their options.
3. Recommending a home-care program helps clients to derive the most benefit from _____ _____.
4. Prescriptive-type memos are an excellent way to communicate _____ directions.
5. A simple format that utilizes generic headings should be followed by _____ that tell the client how and when to use the product.
6. It is a good idea to call clients who receive _____ within 24 hours.
7. Calling back clients takes a considerable amount of _____ and _____.
8. Estheticians are able to work _____ with clients.

Rapid Review Test

Date: _____

Rating: _____

Match the following terms with their descriptions below.

reassure	future purchases	elaborate	clearly	natural part
effectively	individual	motivate	product	communicate

1. The closing consultation is considered to be a _____ of an effective marketing program.
2. _____ explanations may cause further confusion.
3. It is the esthetician's job to _____ and _____ clients and provide them with a(n) _____ program that they can follow on a daily basis.
4. You should _____ your recommendations _____ and _____.
5. A generic prescriptive memo includes a reminder of when to use the _____ and can also be a great reference tool when making _____.

TOPIC 6: TRACKING YOUR SUCCESS

1. Sales are a great way to help estheticians to increase their _____.
2. In some salons, the owner or manager may install a _____ system to stimulate growth.
3. A _____ is a method for gauging the amount of sales and targeting _____ levels.
4. If a quota system is not in place at the salon, it is a good idea to formulate your own _____.
5. Occasionally sales may be _____, depending on market conditions.
6. At some point, you will find that other estheticians will seek your _____. When this happens, you will know that you have met with _____.

Rapid Review Test

Date: _____

Rating: _____

True or False

1. _____ When some managers set sales goals, they will provide incentives for meeting those goals.

2. _____ Sales numbers allow you to take an honest and objective look at your performance.

3. _____ If you are a good esthetician and sales person, your product sales will remain steady throughout the year, no matter what the economy might be.

NOTES

NOTES

NOTES

NOTES

NOTES

NOTES

NOTES

NOTES

NOTES